Contemplation

Copyright© 2021 by Kevin Ernest Hall

All rights reserved. This book is protected by the USA, UK and international copyright laws. This book may not be copied or reprinted for commercial gain or profit. The use of short quotations or occasional page copying for personal or group study is permitted and encouraged. Permission will be granted upon request.

Published by Seraph Creative in 2021
United States / United Kingdom / South Africa / Australia
www.seraphcreative.org

Typesetting & Layout by Feline
www.felinegraphics.com

Printed in USA, UK and RSA, 2021

All rights reserved. No part of this book, artwork included, may be used or reproduced in any matter without the written permission of the publisher.

Print ISBN 978-1-922428-33-2

CONTEMPLATION

An introduction into spiritual
practices of mystical prayer.

KEVIN ERNEST HALL

I would like to delicate this book to Carike Hall, my beautiful wife and life companion.

You helped me see the light when all else was darkness, thank you for teaching me to dream again, believe again, and find Jesus Christ in the moments of life that change our very being.

Thank you for all the editing, hard work, late nights and effort you made making this book possible, may this book help the generations to come to know Jesus Christ as we have come to know Him together.

BEFORE PRAYER

I weave a silence on my lips.
I weave a silence into my mind.
I weave a silence within my heart.
I close my ears to distractions.
I close my eyes to attractions.
I close my heart to temptations.

Calm me O Lord as you stilled the storm
Still me O Lord, keep me from harm
Let all the tumult within me cease
Enfold me Lord in your peace.

David Adam

CONTENTS

Acknowledgements		11
Preface		13
Introduction		15
A Spiritual Practice – Prayer		18
Chapter 1	: Contemplative Prayer	21
Chapter 2	: Quietism	29
Chapter 3	: Hesychasm, "Jesus Prayer"	37
Chapter 4	: Centering Prayer	47
Chapter 5	: Lectio Divina, "Sacred Reading"	53
Chapter 6	: Visio Divina, "Sacred Seeing"	63
Chapter 7	: Silence & Solitude	73
Chapter 8	: Mindfulness	85
Chapter 9	: Detachment	97
Chapter 10	: Examen – the Ignatian way	107
Chapter 11	: "Glossolalia" & "Xenolalia"	117
Chapter 12	: Breathwork	125
Chapter 13	: Psychology of Contemplation	137
Chapter 14	: Philosophy of Contemplation	143
Recommended Reading per Chapter		151
Bibliography		153
About the Author		157

CONTEMPLATION

ACKNOWLEDGEMENTS

To Dr Adonijah Ogbonnaya, as spiritual mentor, and father in the faith, you have changed the course of my life, by your very example and lifestyle. I appreciate all the hours you have poured into my life. You sowed many of the seeds that have now germinated into the garden of ideas that surround me. May this book bless you, as Jesus has blessed me with you.

To Justin & Rachel Abraham, I appreciate you and your family so much, for keeping your love on in the hard moments, saying the things only friends would say, and being an older brother in Christ, teaching me to walk in the fear of the Lord.

To Joseph and Claire Sturgeon, our humble and faithful friends, who have shown us the path of Christ, it's been amazing to learn from your lives, to be shaped by your journey, knowing today, as I write this, your prayers are truly with us.

To Etienne and Hettie Blom, you have become great lights in our journey, thank you for all the advice, prayer and love. Your lives have changed our lives, we appreciate the great gift you are to the body of Christ.

To Chris Blackeby and Linda Lurie being my publishers, I appreciate all the time, patience and effort it takes to work with us. Having your friends cheer you on, like you guys make us feel when we send another book, makes the whole process worthwhile.

To Lou and Elna Maritz, my new parents, I appreciate all your support, care and love for our family. Thank you for making us part of your lives.

To Mom and Dad, I appreciate you both more than words on pages, thank you for standing behind us and cheering us on.

To Nathan and Ryan Hall, my two boys, what a pleasure it has been to see you grow up so quickly, I appreciate and savour every moment with you. Learning to love you as much as the Abba Father loves us, has become my great endeavour.

To you reading this book, a friend in the making, I appreciate the effort and time you are taking to develop your life and secret place with Abba Father, may this next season, be a season where you find more of Him, in every moment of your silent contemplation.

CONTEMPLATION

PREFACE

The story of Christian spirituality cannot be told without contemplation. From its earliest Hebrew background Christian mystical practice has been mostly the result of focused contemplative practices.

Just as in any field of human experience, tools are needed to guide the practitioner to an authentic and proven result in real life. In mystical practices, these are also needed which help guide both the seasoned mystic and the novice on the path. Here in this book Kevin Hall has provided such a tool.

From the first moment I met Kevin in Lenasia, one of the suburbs of Johannesburg South Africa, when he came to hear me teach, I have been conscious of his deep hunger for a deeper spiritual relationship with The Holy One, YHVH through His Son Yeshua or Messiah.

Kevin is a deeply committed contemplative. He has proven himself an effective mystic and continuously delves deeper into the mysteries of the kingdom. He has been studying with me and contributed much to the mystical movement that is filling the earth in this hour.

The question as to how one may navigate the pathways of the realms of the spirit is laid out in this work. By way of contemplation, he has laid in this work, anyone who truly desires can enter the SOD, the mystery of the inner sanctum. If a person desires to take hold of this divine revelation, that person must be willing to persevere through the disciplines of contemplation, a methodology aid here laid out that can help in that journey.

For one who seeks to raise the mood of their soul and vibrate it according to the mysteries of the inner life with God, contemplation is key. Such a one must decide that they are willing to push through the cacophony of voices claiming to have an experience of divinity and find it within themselves.

Kevin has been a persistent practitioner of the mystical life and now lays out for the novice as well as the adept in spirituality, a way to go further and deeper. This is an enriching and transformative work. I commend this book to you.

Adonijah Ogbonnaya
Lake Elsinore, California, April 2021

INTRODUCTION

A devout Protestant, and in some ways Charismatic Christian, I found my faith to have become shallower as time past, my intellectual and spiritual growth seemed stunted.

Although I was able to experience God, and had certain holy moments with God, something was missing. Praying in my "heavenly language" became work and nothing in my faith showed any fruitful change. I had been "saved" for 15 years or more at the time, yet I felt further away from God than ever before.

A spiritual mid-life crisis developed, what the research at Gallup calls, "the middle years"; apparently my experience was not so unique; many Christians experience this same situation at similar timelines on their journey.

At this stage, I met a father of the faith, a Hebrew messianic Jew, a Rabbi. Through his teachings, I learned about practices of faith. One of these practices was a different path of meditation, based on his own years of practice, and his Hebraic background.

I learned that there are methods of prayer also available to Christians who do not share the Catholic faith or the Eastern Orthodox beliefs. Soon I came to a startling realization, we all believed in the same Jesus, we loved God with all our hearts, yet our practices differed greatly.

Somehow, we as protestants, and "Holy Spirit" people, decided to throw the baby, the bath water, and the bath out of the window; leaving us with a faith that held little value for the intellectual path, or even for those who would seek more silence, more contemplation.

My hope and desire in writing this book is to help you along this journey of discovery; to introduce you to the various other methods and practices of our faith that have greatly helped me in my "middle years."

What your Christian doctrine or background might be, is of little consequence to this path. The way forward in our faith is a unity of being: a great work — the work of the body of Christ is now to move forward from our past divisions, and find the strands of truth in our own traditions, and past.

We know the "West" is looking "East"; other systems of faith have infiltrated our culture, our art, and our understanding. As our society becomes more open to these ideas, why not look to our own history, and find where truths are based in our own faith. One should not need to convert to another faith, to gain access to the tried and tested ways of spiritual practice.

In this book, I will be looking at the major developments of the following spiritual practices in Christianity:

- Contemplation
- Centering Prayer
- Breathwork
- Meditation & Mindfulness

We want to understand how these systems of experience have been used in Christianity to delve into the deeper depths of God, and how this has influenced our modern belief systems.

The world is becoming a more spiritual and more emotionally aware planet. This awakening of consciousness is increasing the need for books, literature, and language for our spiritual understanding.

Western Christianity or modern culture has alienated the West from our heritage, and our rich treasure of mystical experience. Most meditative practices have been relegated to eastern belief systems, and foreign concepts.

The church has created so many denominations, so many theological and dogmatic differences, that our ability to see and understand other systems of thinking within our own faith, does not exist. It seems our society has found more wisdom from the East and amalgamated so much more from the secrets of the East, throwing away our history, and our own treasures hidden in the plain sight of history.

Imagine a man, planning to travel to a beautiful place he always admired, looking at the travel books, booking flights and then experiencing the beauty of the place he just visited. This man then returns home to a place he considered drab, and as he comes from the plane to his home, he meets a tourist going back to his country, and in wonder this tourist explains all the beautiful places he had just experienced in the man's own backyard. While listening to the man, he realizes to his own surprise, his luggage is filled with souvenirs from another place, yet he has never bothered to even see half of what this young man just saw in his country.

Let us not be this person, let us be the person of adventure and amazement and wonder for the rich heritage that our fathers and mothers of old have given us. Let us honour this legacy of faith-practices.

A SPIRITUAL PRACTICE – PRAYER

The development of prayer after the initial development of the early church has seen the rise and fall of many vogue ideas, and thoughts on how to appropriately approach this newfound relationship with God.

Many would call this in other terms, "man's search for meaning," I suggest to you this is not just man's search for God, but also God's search for man, finding new ways to deal with humanity after the death of Jesus, and the resurrection of Christ.

The very act of the cross changed the way humanity interacts with divinity. It did not just remove the curtain of separation between God and man; Jesus became the way, the new way, to interact with divinity. Everything we knew in the history of creation changed on that night.

Since the dawn of creation, humanity has tried to deal with God via a sacrificial system, all cultures have in some way implemented a way of interacting with divinity by sacrifices of blood or ritualized systems of interaction. In South America, human sacrifices were the order of the day, in Africa, we interacted with God based on animal sacrifice, the eastern worlds, developed their own blood rites.

Jesus changed everything, no longer was this system needed, He came and demolished a whole human culture based on rituals, and sacrifices; He became the eternal and perpetual sacrifice and helped humanity to change into a somatic one-ness with God.

The human body was transformed by the divine DNA interacting with the genome and building a pathway of relationship and comprehension never before open to the human mind. The change was so drastic, Apostle Paul describes this change as a new species. A whole new interaction interface was created, the human awareness and consciousness were completely changed in those 3 days while Jesus died, and in His resurrection phase, He left a record of ascending and divine increase in frequency and resonance.

This complete dimensional overhaul and change in the human psyche changed the way we are now able to interface with the divine and relate to God in a way never experienced in history since the fall of Adam and Eve in the garden. Everything has changed, yet very few were told, the secret of the torn veil has been kept quiet.

The post-modern culture has now integrated the East with West, the spirituality and history of the East, has captivated the Western mind, and reshaped our understanding of reality. As we rediscover these truths in our own Christianity, and our own history, the heretics of old, have become the voices of the future.

Old ideas: resurfacing and reshaped to this new world, the age of change, Aquarian understanding is being released now, and we have discovered that the roots of our faith are much deeper, much wider than we might have been told.

Some of the old paths as always, the best, they help us to know where to walk, and teach us the old ways, to help us forge our new way forward. The age of change is easier to navigate while using some of the tried and tested ways, and then inventing a few new ones.

As we continue this exploration of contemplation, we will look at spiritual practices within each of the chapters and there is no right or wrong "feeling" in the experience of these practices as you interact with each one.

You will be able to determine which of these spiritual practices suit your temperament, and spiritual style. Most of us have our own spiritual DNA; this means some of the concepts might be foreign, or make you feel uncomfortable, this is normal. You will, however, find the spiritual practice that resonates with you and that practice will become part of your spiritual path as you deepen your relationship with God.

(Celtic Cross)

CONTEMPLATIVE PRAYER

"Contemplative prayer [oración mental] in my opinion is nothing else than a close sharing between friends; it means taking time frequently to be alone with Him who we know loves us."

– St. Teresa of Avila

INFLUENCERS OF CONTEMPLATIVE PRAYER

There are 3 major figures in church history involved in developing the contemplative prayer movement. Although the whole practice was derived from the desert fathers, in the West these three men became the fathers of modern "contemplative prayer," emphasizing different methods, and teachings, their commonality is their view of contemplative prayer.

Evagrius Ponticus was born in Turkey, during 345, in a city then under Roman rule. He was ordained by Basil the Great and in 380 he went to Constantinople where he served as a deacon.

In 383 he became a monk in Jerusalem and lived an ascetic life with little food and sleep. He died in 399 in Scetis, in modern-day Egypt. Although Evagrius accomplished many things in his life, his inclusion in this chapter is due to his recording of the contemplative practices of the desert fathers. He was a disciple of Anthony the Great, and during his time in Egypt tried to record many of these practices. Due to his tireless effort a great legacy was preserved from the desert fathers for the church as a whole.

John Cassian was born in 360 in Dobrogea, Romania. He spent some time with a friend in the Egyptian monastic communities, then fled to Constantinople after a theological controversy. He was ordained after his arrival there. He also spent some time in Rome finding a monastic community there as well as travelling to Antioch.

He then founded a community at Marseilles in 415, the Abbey of St Victor, this community was open to both monks and nuns. John died in 435 at Marseille.

John's method of prayer focuses on developing a pure heart, his practice was also learned from the desert fathers and focuses on the chanting of the psalms. His major work the "Conferences" impacted the church and the leaders like Saint Benedict, and Ignatius of Loyola who both owe their basic ideas to him. His contribution was thus the knowledge base that he was able to transfer to other saints and monks.

John Climacus, whom we will look at in a later chapter needs to be included in this section due to most of his teaching focusing on the simplicity of prayer. He also teaches one to "be present with your every breath," essentially looking at breathing and prayer as one united action.

Who may ascend the mountain of the Lord? Who may stand in his holy place? The one who has clean hands and a pure heart, who does not trust in an idol or swear by a false god.

Psalm 24:4

Essentially all three of these men focused their teaching on the practice of prayer, and the cleansing and purification of the human soul. They all understood the reality of the bible and shared in the teaching of King David as described in Psalm 24.

This purification is not just attained by believing in Christ, and then moving onwards, but a purification of the heart motives, the appropriation of the blood of Jesus into the lives of the saints.

Although we understand we are not saved by our works, the Apostle James does allow for the work of sanctification, which in this case, is performed by the practice of daily devotional commitment to prayer.

CONTEMPLATIVE LIFE

"Living the contemplative life"! What does it refer to when someone says that they are living this life?

The word in the Oxford definition states: "the action of looking thoughtfully at something for a long time." This definition might be accurate, but the reality of living this life is a bit different to express and describe.

Historically the Greek word for contemplation was "Theoria," which means knowledge. The question then becomes how to define what this divine knowledge one receives when in the act of contemplation.

Some have called this process "infused contemplation" due to the divine nature of the practice, unlike the normal act of just contemplating ideas or philosophy. In both the Greek and Latin development of contemplation, the act is described as "to gaze" or "to watch" in some sense creating a practice of spiritual watchfulness, beholding the divine.

The other meaning of the word could be, "being aware of," so in some way cultivating a sense of awareness of the divine presence, intersecting with the material reality.

The journey of contemplation is much like looking into a murky mirror that one must wipe clean. This murkiness is then the way we view ourselves, which is not often a true reflection. This "false self" is an illusion of who we are and must be removed in order for us to see the "true self."

Contemplation is the pursuit of doing the work of thinking about the divine realities of God, and our relationship with the divine, discovering the true self to access the ladder of ascent. This work, to be effective in its nature, needs to take place in the context of understanding that every person has a perspective bias, or cultural conditioning, which clouds the process, and at the core of the journey, dealing with our own ideas, systems of thinking or as some would call it "programs for happiness," is the core function of the contemplative work.

The work of contemplation then brings us to a place where new discoveries can be made, new revelations, new ideas, and thoughts can enter our hearts, as we have dealt with our propensity to judge, condemn, and resolve questions without the proper process or "due process" in legal terms, which should be afforded to the thoughts God wants to reveal.

Let us put this in simpler terms; if God wanted to give you a revelation of Himself, yet this revelation goes against everything you have believed about God before, how will these new revelations penetrate your thinking system?

Living a life of contemplation will ask us to review our belief system.

Creating within us a place of retrospect and enquiring from us to prove the validity of these beliefs. When we allow the contemplative journey to bring these new ideas or revelations to us, we now can accept a newly revealed aspect of God that we once would have discarded.

The contemplative journey requires bravery and perseverance in that it asks of us to look inside and come to terms with the true self. This journey challenges us to peel away the layers of protection and false information about ourselves and our view of the world to come to a place of completion and resolution of many loose ends of the self.

Let us not just engage with the ego and the self; we need to understand the initial goal of contemplation is true awakening, moving from surface-level belief systems, and experiences, to becoming a deep incarnation of Christ Consciousness, and living the life Christ modeled for us, thus becoming the conduit of the divine love, and emanating this love to the people around us.

The pure fire hose of divine love, undiluted, undefiled, gushing forth from the contemplative life. Not living for agendas, hidden motivations, or self-promotion; merely expressing the divine love, as an act of love to God, proving this love, by being proven in the fire of contemplation.

The caution for a contemplative life lies in the immersion of wanting to find the true self at all cost and losing the intentional pursuit of the divine love and the deeper relational connection to God. Forfeiting the outcome of being one with God for becoming a master of self. Let no amount of inner reflection deter the intention of a relationship with God.

Becoming the golden censor of worship, a "vessel of honor" in the living temple of our being. The offensive reality of the "good news": human beings becoming the inflection point, or manifestation where the divine intent finds its materiality and reality.

CONTEMPLATIVE PRAYER

Central to a life of contemplation, is contemplative prayer. The prayer of contemplation can be boiled down to paying attention to the movement of God in the everyday life of the believer.

When we pray all actions and techniques used are there to assist us in focusing our heart and mind on God and letting Him become the sole desire of your being. What some would say a "holy fixation" of attention and intention on the being of God.

The simpler contemplation is, the more real it becomes, the mere focus on wanting a relationship with God, and paying attention to God is in essence the spiritual practice. Contemplation is not about mystical experiences, but simply learning to enjoy the presence of God, and not just a starting point for something else.

The prayer of contemplation is a practice of waiting on God, learning to rest "in God" and then allowing vulnerability and sensitivity to possess the heart and mind, where the love and the presence of God, and His divine love towards us, becomes reality. The process of sensitizing the heart and mind to the moment of God's light, and sometimes fragile touch, on our consciousness.

Contemplative prayer teaches us to delight in Him, enjoying His presence alone, and then developing and open heart that can listen well.

To cultivate this friendship with God, means like any good listener, not to bring our own answers and ideas to the conversation, and then answering the person in our minds before the person is done talking.

In a normal relationship we need to learn to keep our minds quiet, and first hear the person, truly listening to their ideas, views, and thoughts, and only then, we are supposed to propose an answer or a constructive dialogue.

This becomes even more complex when the one speaking to you i.e., God, can hear your thoughts and mind, but is still trying to build relationship with you, even while hearing your cluttering thoughts trying to create noise which makes the communication much harder without silence.

We need to learn to ask God good questions, and then wait for Him, as a good Father, to answer, allowing patience to build a platform in our hearts for God to say something we do not expect. Our own filters and thoughts often limit our ability to hear what God wants to say, which would free us from problems and situations we get entangled with.

A short illustration will help us to create a mental image of what this contemplative prayer looks like in the natural:

When you spend quality time with your husband or wife, you might start with just spending some time chatting about what is going on in your lives, what has been happening that the other person does not know about, this conversation might become deeper as each one talks about the ups and down of life and where you both are at that moment.

There could be some tears, some laughter! This togetherness creates a space of listening, giving encouragement and guidance. Then, after all is said, the conversation will fall into a stillness of just being together, of having been heard, of talking about solutions. And in that moment of silence, you are just resting in each other's presence, finding comfort in the love, and experiencing peace. This then, is contemplation and prayer.

THE PRACTICE OF CONTEMPLATIVE PRAYER

The practice of contemplative prayer is very much interlinked with the life of contemplation and there are various techniques to use. We will look at a classic contemplative prayer practice to get us started in this pathway of contemplation.

Consider this phrase John Cassian recommended in his teaching from Psalm 70:1 –

> *"O God, make speed to save me: O Lord, make haste to help me"*

Or

> *"Come quickly and rescue me!, God, show me your favor and restore me." (Passion translation)*

The practice then relates to repeating this sentence for about 15 min per day, as a start, just simply repeating the phrase, not trying to find meaning, or theological ideas. You will feel the gaze of your mind try to look or think about other matters, simply remain calm and repeat the phrase.

We understand from the bible, God is seated in heaven, before Him is a "sea like glass," let us imagine this sea is our emotions, and let us consider then to sit in a position of spiritual rest, seated above our emotions.

You will notice if you have been stressed, your emotions might become agitated, I often use this seat of rest technique to calm my emotions, to slow down my breathing, until I see that the ocean of emotion in my mind is calming.

I use these techniques, as ways to visualize emotional dis-ease, and then change the churning waters of my body, which became agitated, to come to rest, and allow for effective contemplation.

God gave us an imagination; we can use it. When things are really going crazy, sometimes I even use the sound of water, and then slowly change the sound from a storm to a calm sea, to allow my mind, and my heart to synchronize the reality of the outer world, with my inner world.

Once the "sea" is calm in my heart, I then allow my thoughts to repeat the exercises.

Please pay attention to the moments in your daily life that create the propensity for the water in your body to become upset. We all get stressed at work, or with people, however, the key is to find the trigger point, what exactly is causing this inner storm.

Once this has been identified, one can then start the physiological process of analyzing those feelings and learning why you are feeling the way you are feeling, and how the actions of people outside of you have been allowed to drive your internal reality. Fears of rejection, failure or insecurity often undergird some of these emotional responses.

As you continue to practice on a regular basis the words of Psalm 70 verse 1 will become ingrafted into your memory and you will be able to lean on those experiences in your quiet time when moments of turmoil arise in your day.

Your quiet time will become quieter as you resolve these emotional triggers and you will come to a posture of stillness that becomes a conduit for the presence of God to infill, surround and comfort you.

(Spanish Cross)

QUIETISM

Devotional contemplation and abandonment of the will as a form of religious mysticism. A state of passive quietness.

INFLUENCERS OF QUIETISM

"With the wind of tribulation God separates in the floor of the soul, the chaff from the corn."

-- Miguel de Molinos

One cannot discuss the ideas of quietism, without speaking about Miguel de Molinos, a true revolutionary on prayer. His prayer method set the church alight and moved from Spain to Italy and France.

Miguel was a controversial figure, born in 1628, he was close to Zaragoza in Spain and later moved to Valencia. In 1675 he published his famous work the "Spiritual Guide." Some historians called him a "spiritual genius"; a man born before his time.

During the Spanish Inquisition, Miguel was sentenced to life imprisonment due to his "doctrinal error," according to the Pope at the time. Miguel died in December 1696, in what I believe to be one of the saddest errors in the history of the church.

When we kill our revolutionaries and our theological innovators, our voice in society becomes dull in the ears of a saturated culture. His work was the beginning of the practice of Quietism and inspired many after him to pursue the practice and add to the development thereof.

Francois Fenelon was one of a few major thinkers in France following this quietist philosophy and appreciating the new avenues of spiritual growth which would be available during the time.

He was born in 1651 to a noble family, in Sainte-Mondane, France. Francois's family had a long history in the church, his uncles and family members were well-known church leaders.

In 1675 he was ordained as a priest, and in 1686-1687 he served the church as a missionary to the protestant Huguenots in the south of France. He had a great love for the Huguenots and persuaded the King to reduce troops and end violent shows of persecution.

In 1688 he met with Jeanne Guyon, his first cousin, impressed by her devotion, and her method of prayer, he defended her concepts of quietism vehemently to the church, as he saw her method of prayer and contemplation to build character and move into unity with Christ. They wrote a book together that included the practice of Quietism and this recorded work gave more legitimacy to quietism.

Although most historians will not include George Fox in the quietism movement, his ideas and method look and sound remarkably familiar to the movement of the Holy Spirit in revealing quietism as a spiritual path.

Born on 1624 in Leicestershire England, to a wealthy weaver family. As a child, he was seen to be spiritually inclined. His father died in 1650 and left him with a substantial inheritance which allowed him the time to pursue his spiritual path.

He was not formally educated, but proclaimed to be led by the Holy Spirit, and the inner voice of God speaking and educating Him in the divine path. He read the Bible with great enthusiasm and tried to find priests that could help educate him. He gave up this search and started reading and searching the scriptures himself for the answers his soul longed for.

At the age of 23 he started preaching what God had shown him. He preached against formalism, and dead spiritual works.

While he was preaching, people came to tease and mock him, and he started shaking and quaking uncontrollably, hence the nickname "Quakers" came to be their calling card. His contribution to the concept and practice of quietism, was in the creation of a movement of people that practiced this form of Quietism.

QUIETISM AND ITS MAIN CONCEPTS

Quietism is a "prayer of quiet" where the focus and intent are more important than outward actions and words. The "prayer of quiet" is an internal prayer or "silent" prayer focused on a singular idea or concept of Jesus. Teresa of Avila, coining the phrase "prayer of quiet," preferred to focus her silent prayer on the wounds of Christ.

The roots of quietism might sound almost like passivism, and the abandonment of action, to simply be present; however, the intent of this silent prayer is the pivotal element to create the connection point to the divine. The silent prayer directs the prayer to internalize the focus of the prayer, to turn outside noise and actions to an inward actualization.

One of the major schools of thought with regards to quietism is that all efforts the soul makes to approach God are completely useless, and all action is vanity, and although I do not share this view, I do believe there is something to be said for still, quiet contemplation.

Another belief in this movement speaks to the idea that all thoughts, all desires, all effort carries no value, one needs to be completely silent, quiet the mind, the soul and the whole being of the person, only then can the Divine be approached with no human efforts.

I believe this might be overreaching the reality of materiality, almost believing that human existence itself to become an offense to God, an idea that dismisses the very reality of God creating us and the continued influence that God has in our lives.

The last major concept I would like to address is thoughts on "inner listening" associated with the Quakers, taught by George Fox, yet seemingly similar to the practice of quietism.

From this movement, we learn your "inner light" or the "light of Christ within" is more important than the outward teachings, actions, and external leavers of control by society.

> *The true light that gives light to everyone was coming into the world.*
> **John 1:9 (NIV)**

> *"Art thou in the darkness? Mind it not, for if thou dost it will feed thee more. But stand still, and act not, and wait in patience, till light arises out of darkness and leads thee."*
> **James Nayler**

This light inside of us, the presence of God, that illuminates the way forward, as David wrote in **Psalm 119:105** – *"Your word is a lamp for my feet, a light on my path"*.

This practice of allowing the "inner light of Christ" to guide and teach us then brings us face to face with our own brokenness and wrong motivations, and then moves and motivates us towards the divine solution.

The light of Christ illuminates the path, not just a path of resolution, but also a way of serving the community, and serving the body of Christ as community. One could easily dismiss the Quaker way, however, looking at their achievements in society, and all their active results and the fingerprint of God they left on the West, it would be hard to dismiss their experience as mere fanciful tales.

These ideas and teachings within quietism give us an indication of the practices that we as modern-day believers can include in our daily walk with God. Below are the practices that I believe could be of value to us to explore:

- Letting Go of Anxiety
- Cultivating Silence
- Inner Calm
- Inner Realties and Reflection
- Inward Silence
- Prayer of Surrender

QUESTIONABLE CONCEPTS THAT STEMMED FROM QUIETISM

In any new approach to something or revelation received, there is discernment needed to determine the validity and biblical truth in the matter. The early church, however, had already condemned this movement as heretical and the practice of quietism was relinquished in fear of losing control of how people experienced the divine.

However, I believe the time has come for us to extract from quietism, the practices that are biblically true and that extol the fundamental longing for a deeper connection with the divine. When the Holy Spirit emphasizes a spiritual truth, which is then taken too far out of context, the typical "pendulum swing," it removes the beauty from what was originally intended.

Some of the questionable concepts in quietism are:

- The idea that all action is evil
- Passivity as spirituality
- Procrastination seen as holy
- Inactivity seen as divine spirituality

This is clearly not what the Bible teaches. Let us look at some biblical examples:

> *"What does it profit, my brethren, if someone says he has faith but does not have works? Can faith save him? If a brother or sister is naked and destitute of daily food, and one of you says to them, "Depart in peace, be warmed and filled," but you do not give them the things which are needed for the body, what does it profit? Thus also faith by itself, if it does not have works, is dead."*
> **James 2:14-26**

I believe all types of prayer have intrinsic value, not just in building a relationship with God, but also in the manner in which it changes our soul and spirit. Any communication between us and God is desirable to God, He wants a relationship with us and that includes communication.

To elevate silence above speech, is clearly not what happened in the life of Jesus. When His own disciples asked him to teach them how to pray, Jesus prayed the "Our Father," loudly and with the intention to teach a method of prayer, which was vocal in nature.

Despite these objections, the movement of quiet prayer has brought a wonderful focus to prayer, which was needed in the time of its birth in the middle ages; and I contend, that this focus on prayer, is once again needed in this day and hour. Let us not throw away the gold with the dirt and proclaim all as useless.

> *"Therefore, thus says the LORD, "If you return, then I will restore you-- Before Me you will stand; And if you <u>extract the precious from the worthless</u>, You will become My spokesman. They for their part may turn to you, But as for you, you must not turn to them."*
> **Jerimiah 15:19 (NASB)**

CONTEMPLATION

THE PRACTICE OF QUIETISM

Now that we understand where this movement comes from, what the historical trends were, and some of the concepts each of its proponents taught their followers, let us continue onto the actualization of quietism in our daily lives.

Before we delve into a practice, we need to remember that the concept of silent prayer is rooted in silence. The world has become a noisy place and we need to learn how to be silent again. Thus saying; some of the practices throughout the book will challenge you to become silent and to look inward and to drown out the noises. But the reward will be such a blessing to you as you experience God in this new way of peace and tranquility.

The practice of quietism is the practice of silence. How each person achieves a place of silence around and in themselves is dependent upon their previous engagement with contemplation. We will thus look at a very introductory practice that can easily be expanded as we grow into quietism and become more comfortable with silence.

Let us first read a poem by Ann Lewin about silence and find the points of intersection with the practice we will follow.

> You do not have to
> Look for anything,
> Just look.
>
> You do not have to
> Listen for specific sounds,
> Just listen.
>
> You do not have to
> Accomplish anything
> Just be.
>
> And in the looking,
> And the listening,
> And the being,
> Find Me.

Becoming Still:

- Find a quiet place
- Be comfortable
- Pray internally
- Just look
- Just listen
- Just be
- Write down any reflections

Our internal prayer of silence needs to have a focus. We started our discussion on quietism with the emphasis on the intent of the prayer. Our intent will be the stabilizer in the prayer; as we pray and other thoughts distracts from the intent, we can easily bring the prayer back into the intent and in so doing also create this safe space within ourselves to connect with God.

(Orthodox Cross)

HESYCHASM

CHAPTER 3

Hesychasm is an inner awareness and focus on prayer, contemplating and using the invocation of the name of Jesus, consistently repeating His holy name, as a practice of complete union with God. The one using this practice avoids the external impulses, and completely becomes immersed in the inner reality of Christ abiding in the heart of the believer.

INFLUENCERS OF HESYCHASM

"The offspring of virtue is perseverance. The fruit and offspring of perseverance is habit and child of habit is character."

— St. John Climacus

John Climacus was born in Syria in 579. Around the age of 40, he lived at the Sinai Monastery, he later died in Egypt at the monastery. John was the Saint who introduced the use of the word "hesychasm" into society due to the popularity of his famous work, Ladder of Divine Ascent.

Before this time, the concept was used sparingly and interchanged with other concepts relating to "divine quietness".

There is almost no information about John Climacus, due to the early nature of his life, the records in this period are quite hard to find. It is noted he served at Mount Sinai "Vatos Monastery" at the foot of mount Sinai, in Egypt.

His writings speak of a quality education, which he would have needed to attain elsewhere, some believe he started at the monastery at the age of 16, however this is disputed by most modern scholars, due to the references in his writing.

It seems that he lived in Gaza, where he practiced law; after the death of his wife, he moved to the monastery at Sinai, at the age of 40. John was reputed for his understanding and wisdom. This led to Gregory the

Great sending him money for a local hospital when he was 65 years of age.

His work, Ladder of Divine Ascent centered around the idea that you must work through 30 steps to attain an ascetic lifestyle. The first 7 steps in the ladder speaks about character traits one needs to have for the ascetic lifestyle. The next 19 steps teach the reader how to overcome sinful bents in character, and how to develop a foundational ascetic character. The last 4 steps teach on the higher virtues of the ascetic lifestyle and the aim of the pursuit of heavenly virtues or character traits. The final and last step or rung of the "ladder of divine ascent", then culminates in love, the highest attainment of the mystic living an ascetic life.

John aimed this work as a training manual for monks, however, it soon became a seminal work of the Eastern Orthodox and Byzantine Catholic Christianity, widely read by the members of the whole body and in so doing, the concept of hesychasm became familiar and more widely used and turned into a practice of contemplation.

Another Saint that practiced this form of contemplation was Saint Nicephorus. What we know about Saint Nicephorus is due to his tutelage of St Gregory. Saint Nicephorus was known to be an Italian from Greece, either Sicily or Calabria, he traveled to Constantinople and settled there, converting from Roman Catholic to the Eastern Orthodox church.

Due to his opposition to the union of these two churches at the Synod of Lyon in 1274, he was subjected to imprisonment.

After his release, he traveled to Mount Athos and lived at the hermitage at Karyes, this is where he wrote his most famous work "On the Watchfulness and Guarding of the Heart."

He was also known as The Hesychasm, mostly due to his devotion to the practice and his teaching about the practice thereof in conjunction with breathing.

> "You know that our breathing is the inhaling and exhaling of air. The organ that serves for this is the lungs that lie round the heart, so that the air passing through them thereby envelops the heart. Thus, breathing is a natural way to the heart. And so, having collected your mind

within you, lead it into the channel of breathing through which air reaches the heart and, together with this inhaled air, force your mind to descend into the heart and to remain there."

– Saint Nicephorus

One of the most notable saints in history, Gregory Palamas, also taught on this subject and was considered a master in the practice of Hesychasm.

Gregory Palamas was born in Constantinople in 1296, to a noble family, his family had duties in the senate. His father died early and the Emperor at the time took an interest in him and tried to advance his education. Although the expectation was for him to enter government service, he decided to become a monk.

He started his monastic journey at Mount Athos. He studied with Theoleptus of Philadelphia, who taught him the prayer of the heart, and the ways of the church. He spent time in a monastery at Vatopedi, here he was directed by Elder Nicodemus.

After the death of his brother and his mentor, he moved to the Monastery of the Great Lavra, where he conducted his duties as chanter. He accomplished many feats due to his practice, staying awake for 3 months without sleep. He then moved to the hermitage of Glossia, to seek silence, and to be subject to the teachings of Gregory of Byzantium.

In 1326, he was ordained as a priest and started a hermitage around Beroea. When his mother died, he went back to Constantinople (modern-day Istanbul) to fetch his sisters and then returned to Mount Athos, secluding himself at in the hermitage of Saint Savas, where he had many divine visions, and experiences.

In 1335, he became the Abbot of the Monastery of Esphigmenou. After trying to teach the 200 monks for a year, he returned to the silence of his hermitage. He died in Thessalonica on November 14, 1359, after a long illness, caused by his earlier capture by the Turks, where he spoke to the Muslim clergy and philosophers.

Gregory's major contribution to Hesychasm was his defense of the practice against Barlaam and his philosophical humanism. Barlaam was on a mission to discredit the practice because of his intellectual approach to theology. Gregory wrote nine papers in response to this attack on Hesychasm as requested by the monks that used the practice.

During the time that Gregory defended the practice and gave testimony to the fact he was charged with heresy by the church, however, this was mostly a political move by The Patriarch, John Calecas, due to the civil war at the time.

At the third council of the church in 1351, Gregory was vindicated, and his doctrine was used as the rule of faith of the Orthodox church. Hesychasm remained a practice approved by the church.

HESYCHASM AND "THE JESUS PRAYER"

Although Hesychasm and "the Jesus Prayer" are interchangeable, there are some other interpretations or related terms traditionally also known as hesychasm. These include:

- Proseuche (inner attention)
- Nepsis (watchfulness)
- Mneme theou (memory of God)
- Phylaki kardia (guarding the heart)

We will thus be using the reference to "the Jesus Prayer" as we continue our journey as this is the specific practice of Hesychasm that we want to introduce.

The aim of the practice is unceasing prayer, and developing a heart of humility toward God, without the use of images and imagination. The mind is silenced by the repeated prayer; by praying the Jesus prayer, the process becomes a practiced repetition, almost automatically repeated while you are busy with your normal daily life. The practice can also be called the process of purification of the heart.

I would like to tell you of my first few experiences of praying the prayer, and what happened while I was praying as a starting point to the practice of "the Jesus Prayer."

I initially just spent alone time in my study at home; praying "the Jesus Prayer" with my limited understanding of what the prayer was about and how to best practice the prayer and incorporate it into my life. I approached it like schoolwork, repetition upon endless repetition. But it was one of the most boring times in my life, it was a huge struggle, every moment was like a torture chamber of repeating a single line that did not feel like it changed me.

A few years into the process, I went on my first meditation retreat in Spain; it was a special time of discovery and re-discovery. At the time I was not praying "the Jesus Prayer" as much as I did in the past; however, the practice stayed with me.

A few days before the start of the retreat, we traversed the various pilgrimage routes and sites in the area where we stayed and just pulled on the history of pilgrimage in Spain, engaging with every aspect and allowing Holy Spirit to guide us as we moved.

One particular road we took, led us to an old church monastery on the coast of the Mediterranean, like a light beacon, welcoming us to explore its history. The monastery was large and beautiful as it looked from a height in the mountain to the see below. It had pathways around the monastery and as we climbed a little hill at the back of the monastery, I could feel the prayer suddenly bubble up inside of me.

As I walked on the path I started praying "the Jesus Prayer." I had prayer beads in my hand and used them to help me pace the prayer as the atmosphere shifted and my heart became overwhelmed. I was taken into a vision of the past, where monks and priests walked this path and prayed this prayer. The prayer of Jesus revibrated on their lips, and the very nature of God filled the vision. I could sense the holy fear and awe of God surrounding them.

My eyes filled with tears, and on this silent hill, something inside me changed; the practice that felt laborious, and dry, became a river of joy, a spring of glory, filling the edges of my heart.

THE PRACTICE OF THE JESUS PRAYER

The simplicity of the practice, and the complete focus this requires seems easy and quite mundane, however, beneath this ancient practice, lies an avenue of prayer, that few other traditions can mimic.

You could ask me, why would you want to repeat the same words for hours, constantly saying the same thing, it must be the most boring and soul-numbing act one could think about.

You would be right, and in some way, this is exactly the point, driving the mind and the soul to complete boredom, and contemplating the hidden truth of the words over and over drives a deeper meaning, a deeper experience of the words, into a place of reality.

Although the prayer itself is not there to help you think about the theology of the matter and to fill your mind with "explanation" of the prayer while you partake in the practice, please indulge me in some thoughts on the prayer to show that there is complexity beneath the surface and bring to light the depth of understanding that the Saints had about their relationship with the divine. This will encourage us to look deeper into our hearts and embrace the sacrifice of Christ.

"LORD JESUS CHRIST, SON OF GOD, HAVE MERCY ON ME, A SINNER"

1) **Lord Jesus** – Who is Jesus? The man on the cross, the God-Man on the cross, the man who was pierced 7 times, who is this man, what was His pain, how did He suffer?

2) **Christ** – the Christ, slain before the foundation, as John writes. Who is this Christ, the Savior of the world, the lamb slain before creation? Who is this lamb, why would He, as part of God, allow His existence to be taken from Him, being already part of the trinity? How was He slain, how was He removed from the trinity, to allow death into His being?

3) **Son of God** – What does this son mean, begotten yet not born; how did He exist before His "sonship,", or was He always a son?

4) **Have Mercy on Me** – What is mercy, and since I do not deserve this mercy by any action of my own, how do I obtain mercy? What do I need mercy for, what are my many shortcomings I am asking mercy for? Why do I need mercy, if God created me, and knew my shortcomings, am I to blame for my weakness, why do I need mercy in the first place?

5) **A sinner** – This is not an admission of a permanent state of being, but rather a declaration of the need of salvation, the need of the believer to be in permanent receiving of mercy, for shortcomings.

As you notice from the questions and thinking patterns, the prayer becomes a method of meditating on Jesus Christ, and thus flows into the life of the believer the ability to move from the current state of existence to a more elevated thinking pattern.

This is a basic contemplation on "the Jesus Prayer"; however, as one spends more time praying the prayer, the avenues of prayer open up to vistas of exploration and discovery.

The result is then the movement from mere contemplative prayer, and meditation of the words, to a repetitive reprogramming of the subconscious mind, providing a system of thinking constantly ruminating on the thoughts of the divine.

We all have thought patterns, ideas, and repetitive thoughts, mostly negative, and often based on fear, or past traumatic experiences. The practice of this prayer starts us on the journey of learning to re-program those thoughts, and create a positive thinking system, which enables the unconscious mind, to become transformed via repetition.

The process of transformation of the mind has often been attempted by mere memorization of scripture verses, however, this laborious process, often just focuses on the aware mind, the conscious mind of the believer, requiring active thinking processes, which is not always possible in the routine of living.

The process of "the Jesus Prayer," by the very nature of the constantly repeating of the prayer, and frustrating the cognitive process, starts to short circuit the normal pathways of thinking into the exploration of God, into a more immersive experience.

Our ability to learn methods of dealing with the mind, building systems of thinking not just on the Western linear process, but an eastern circular system developed by the Hebraic mind, and transferred to the Syrian and Egyptian church fathers, we make use of to re-discover the process of using the rhythm of life, and natural flow of life, building prayer patterns into this flow, and then allowing the flow of these prayers to impact us on a much deeper level than mere cognitive memory techniques.

We also need to understand that most movements in prayer, require the impact of the God on the person, unlike many self-help methods which mimic these practices. As Christians we believe God to be present in our search for Him, we assume the work of the divine in our practice, which allows for higher levels of growth and change, due to the enablement of the divine, energizing the soul into the process of maturing.

PRACTICAL ADVICE

To start the exploration of the prayer, find a quiet place where you can pray, away from people, phones, and the world. Say "the Jesus Prayer" loud enough so your ears can hear the words – slowly focusing on each word.

The spacing of the words could be as follows:

**Lord .... Jesus Christ .... Son of God ....
Have Mercy .... On Me .... A Sinner**

You can say the words as they suit your own pace, just make sure you are deliberate and intentional in your execution.

When you reach the end of the prayer, start saying it again, you can also increase or decrease your pace to help you focus on the words. Just focus on the words, sometimes slow down to each syllable, other times, say the prayer as fast as you can, without the words melting into each other.

If your minds wonder, do not think that you are not able to do this. We are all in a process of learning and cultivating this practice. Bring your thoughts back to the prayer and continue praying.

Things to Avoid:

- Do not try to visualize the image of Jesus.
- Do not contemplate the life of Jesus, or theology of Jesus.
- Do not focus on yourself, or your sins.

Helpful Tips:

- Aim to pray 15 min per day, working upwards to 30min per day.
- Preferably pray in the mornings when you are awake.
- You will get sleepy, get up, prostrate yourself before God.
- Get some prayer beads or a prayer rope, it helps to keep those fingers from fiddling.

(Russian Cross)

CENTERING PRAYER

"Prayer of the Heart"

Centering Prayer is a method of meditative prayer placing a strong emphasis on interior silence where the focus moves from external methods of prayer into a responsive prayer of resting in God for the purpose of a personal relationship with God.

INFLUENCERS OF CENTERING PRAYER

"Silence is God's first language; everything else is a poor translation."

– Thomas Keating

The Centering Prayer movement was started by Fr. William Meninger, an American Trappist monk, born and raised in Boston Massachusetts. His mother was born and raised in Ireland, and his father was a Quaker from Pennsylvania.

After studying at St John's Seminary in Boston, he became an ordained priest in 1958. Deeply influenced by the 14th Century English hermit who wrote "Cloud of Unknowing." He developed his own system of contemplation to make this practice more available to people wanting to practice contemplation.

In 1974 he held his first workshop, which became centering prayer focusing on forgiveness, prayer, and the sacred scriptures. He influenced his abbot at the time, Basil Pennington, and Thomas Keating, who would later become an advocate of centering prayer, and create greater momentum in America for the practice of centering prayer.

Thomas Keating was born in New York in March 1923. He attended Deerfield Academy, Yale University, and Fordham University where he completed his education. In St. Joseph's Abbey, Spencer, Massachusetts, he met William Meninger, leading to his interest in the practice of centering prayer.

In 1984 Thomas Keating co-founded Contemplative Outreach, Ltd. This organization ushered in a safe place for the learning and practice of among other methods, Centering Prayer!

The third party to the then developing practice of centering prayer was Basil Pennington. He was born in 1931, in Brooklyn NY. He received degree from Cathedral College of the Immaculate Conception, in 1951 at which time he entered the Order of Cistercians, where he followed the strict Trappist tradition.

He was ordained as a priest in 1957 at St. Joseph's Abbey in Spencer, Massachusetts, where he met William Meninger and Thomas Keating. These three priests are seen as the founders of centering prayer moments in the USA, although the tradition was taken from the contemplative prayer roots much earlier in the history of Europe.

The three monks would develop this method of prayer and offer it to the lay community of the Catholic church as a spiritual practice, the movement has never stopped growing.

Although Thomas Merton was not involved in the centering prayer movement, his life certainly foreshadowed what would later become a tide of contemplation and change the face of Catholicism and Christianity in the West.

Born in the Pyrenees France on January 31, 1915 to Owen Merton, a New Zealand painter, and Ruth Jenkins, an American artist and quaker by faith. His mother died when he was six years old. His father had him baptized in England. He moved between New York (Queens), France and England frequently.

In 1931 his father died after which he started his studies at Cambridge in 1933. This period at Cambridge was not a happy time in his life, often in legal troubles, and fathering a child he never met. His father's friend then suggested to him to study at Columbia University where he would start in 1935.

His mentor Mark van Doren, led him to read some spiritual masterpieces, and helped him discover his spiritual path. In 1939 he was received into the catholic church, and soon after wanted to become a priest. He became a Trappist monk at the abbey of Gethsemane, and under the direction of the abbot, wrote the "Seven Story Mountain" which later became a New York best-selling book.

Merton was believed to have used the term "Centering Prayer" first. Below is his teaching on centering prayer, in a very brief description, please take note he was one of the thought leaders at this time, so there is a huge amount of material available to learn from his teaching.

Summary of Merton's 7 Stages of Centering Prayer:

1) Silence - Consenting to God's Presence
2) Solitude - Disregarding our Interior Dialogue and Resting in God
3) Solidarity - Awareness of Increasing "One-ness"
4) Service - God in Us, Serving the God in Others
5) Stillness - Presence Beyond Rational Concepts
6) Simplicity - Integration of Contemplation and Action
7) Surrender - Abiding State of the Soul from Unity to Union with the Divine

CENTERING PRAYER AS A PRACTICE

Centering prayer is in essence the practice of "letting go" of thoughts in the flow of our conscious awareness and allowing an open heart and mind towards God, empty of the self but filled with the presence of God.

This practice teaches the mind to be less attached to thoughts and ideas generated by life and experiences, and simply allow them to pass, observing the thoughts as an objective bystander, and then moving into the interior silence of the presence of God.

Central to the practice of centering prayer is choosing a "sacred word" that one uses to center or focus the mind as one sits silently with a receptive posture. When we then become aware of thoughts, emotions, or feelings, the "sacred word" is vocalized to allow the thoughts to become still again. It is not used unceasingly, only as required.

The "sacred word" is any word that you connect to God, that will help your mind to focus on quieting the soul. This word can be interchanged with other words in different sessions. For example, if you practice in the morning, a word like "grace" or "mercy" might help you to prepare for the day ahead, but a practice in the evening could engage a word like "thankful" or "holy" to end your day.

Examples of words:

> **Love ... Grace ... Joy ... Peace ... Light ... Heart ... Yes ...
> Be ... Now ... Life ... Hope ... Faith ... Jesus ... Christ ...
> Holy ... Still ... Spirit ... Father ... Mother ... Heaven ...
> Glory**

The "sacred word" expresses our intention and then starts to affect the attention of the mind. The purpose of this prayer is to learn absolute surrender and letting go of the ego, giving oneself to God. It becomes the access point where we allow the gentle Holy Spirit to enter our mind, via our will, and using the sacred word to express our will, to intentionally seek God.

The "sacred word" is not magical, it is merely like a switch, allowing our awareness to focus, and congeal the intention into a simple word or syllable.

This practice of inner silence becomes our participation with God, this sacred silent space inside us becomes the intersection with divinity and our humanity.

THE PRACTICE OF CENTERING PRAYER

The essential being and purpose of all prayer is connection with the divine. The aim therefore of this practice is to inspire some form of enthusiasm for silent prayer and to translate the ideas into our busy lives.

Centering prayer is an easier entry into the world of contemplations and when done regularly becomes an intuitive practice for reaching out to God in every situation. You will learn how to quiet your mind even when you do not have access to a still place. The very act of centering prayer is the movement from outside, to inside, to God.

THE METHOD:

1. Choose a quiet place to posture yourself.
2. Decide on a "sacred word" which reflects your intention to consent and connect to God's presence e.g., God, Love, Jesus.
3. Focus your intention for the prayer in your mind.
4. Use the "sacred word" as an expression of intention towards God's presence by verbally saying it.
5. When thoughts rush in, focus on the "sacred word," and repeat the "sacred word" slowly.
6. At the end of the prayer session, remain in the same position and posture, and remain quiet for a few minutes.
7. Remember that this is also a receptive time for receiving from God.

This method of prayer focuses the intention of the prayer. There is a strong emphasis on the passion of the heart, and intention and desire within. Therefore, this prayer form is sometimes called "Heartfulness."

We learn to hear the voice of our inner being, and then allow our thoughts or unspoken ideas, our hidden motivations to rise to the surface, allowing us to deal with our hidden agendas, and move along our journey with God. Our heart can be comforted in this prayer and life can fill the hurt and dead places within that space.

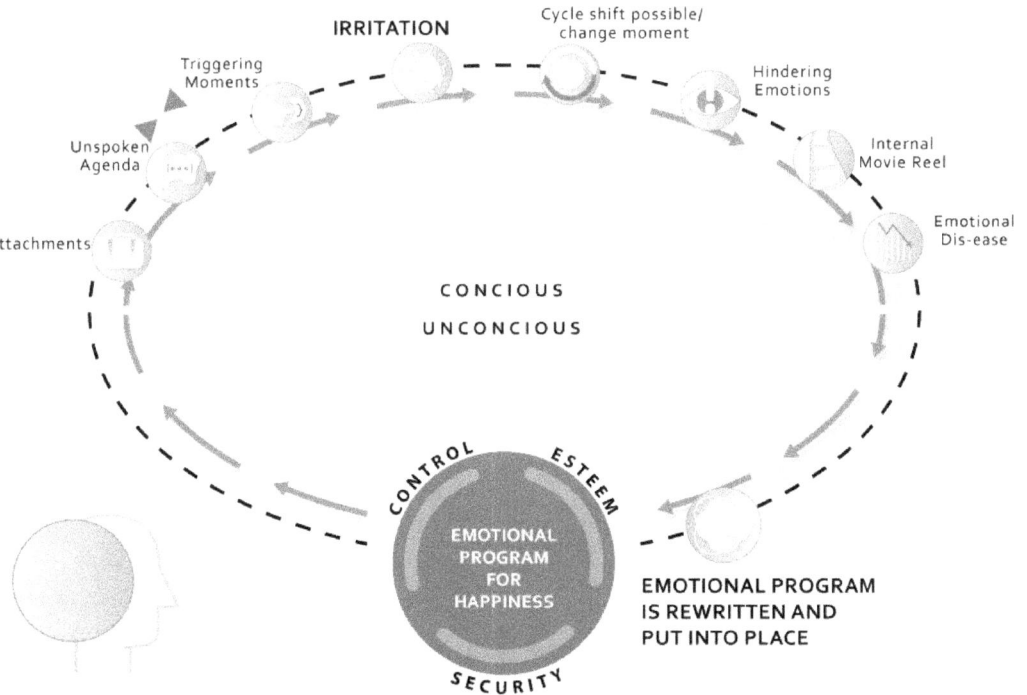

(Syrian Cross)

LECTIO DIVINA:

"divine reading"

Lectio Divina flows out of the Hebrew method of studying the Scriptures which is called *Haggadah or learning by the heart*. Haggadah was an interactive interpretation of the Scriptures by means of the free use of the text to explore its inner meaning. (Spirituality and Practice)

INFLUENCERS OF LECTIO DIVINA

Origen Adamantius was born in 184, in Alexandra, Egypt. His father instilled in him a love for the bible, and he memorized various passages from an early age. He was well read on a number of subjects, but his love for theology landed him a position at the School of Alexandria, where he lectured on theology.

Origen converted a wealthy benefactor, Ambrose. He was so impressed by Origen that he sponsored his studies and paid for all his writing to be published. He also provided Origen with seven writers and secretaries to help him write and take note of his theology and ideas.

Origen is a controversial figure in church history, due to his disagreements with Demetrius, the bishop of Alexandria, and some of his theological views. His huge canon of work has always been a major contribution to Christian theology.

In the 3rd Century Origen, began to explore the idea that scripture has some hidden allegorical meaning and interpretation. Meaning there is more to the bible than the face value literal translation of the Hebrew and Greek into English.

Origen proposed one should let the scripture "touch" the reader, by allowing the words and the meaning to linger, and reading the divine scripture privately and loudly, to help understand this hidden meaning.

One of Origen's main ideas reads as follows, *"Scriptura sui ipsius Interpres"*; Scripture is its own interpreter. Thus, the process of sacred reading follows this idea to the end.

Pope Gregory I born in 540, in Rome, Italy, was also a major teacher and proponent of Lectio Divina. He was well known for his work regarding the liturgy of the church at that time. He sent a mission to England to convert them and built relationships with many in Europe at that time.

He wrote, *"The biblical Scriptures are letters from Almighty God to his creatures. The Lord of all has sent you his letters for your life's advantage—and yet you neglect to read them eagerly. Study them, I beg you, and meditate daily on the words of your Creator. Learn the heart of God in the words of God" (Letters, 5, 46).*

Due to this focus on the sacred scripture, he admonishes the church to meditate and think on the scripture, Lectio Divina would be the way of meditation.

Saint Benedict was an interesting character born in 480 in Italy. He founded twelve monasteries in Italy. He created a rule in his monastic system for "scriptural reading," to allow God to speak to the monks and the church.

St Benedict quotes scripture about the "living nature" or "living word" reality allowing the bible to read us, the children of the Master Jesus.

> *But what saith it? The word is nigh thee, even in thy mouth, and in thy heart: that is, the word of faith, which we preach; That if thou shalt confess with thy mouth the Lord Jesus, and shalt believe in thine heart that God hath raised him from the dead, thou shalt be saved. For with the heart man believeth unto righteousness; and with the mouth confession is made unto salvation.*
>
> **Romans 10:8-10**

> *For the word of God is quick, and powerful, and sharper than any two-edged sword, piercing even to the dividing asunder of soul and spirit, and of the joints and marrow, and is a discerner of the thoughts and intents of the heart.*
>
> **Hebrews 4:12**

LECTIO DIVINA AND THE SACRED SCRIPTURE

Every faith has its own "sacred scriptures," which they believe were given by God to humanity, to light the path towards spiritual growth and knowledge of the divine.

Christianity believes the bible to be this sacred book, not just a work of literature, but a sacred book, where the words written, are the very words of God, inspired and given to holy men to write, as God speaks to humanity.

Whether you read the Ethiopian bible, with 88 books or the Western versions of the bible, the fact is, the scripture is still sacred, and still contains the word of God. We understand scripture is not inerrant, there are mistakes made due to the transmission of such an ancient work, humans needed to copy by hand, every word written.

We must remember that scripture cannot contain God! Even if we believe the scripture to be the words of God to humanity, no scripture or human writing can contain a God who created everything and made us His children. We should rather approach the bible, as God's letter to us, as humanity, and then interpret and question the scriptures from this place.

In Jewish tradition, the scripture is considered the mouthpiece of God, with multiple dimensions of interpretation and understanding.

We can, however, believe the words written in this beautiful, ancient book contain the very thoughts of God, the ideas of Divinity, communicated to humanity. Thus, the way we approach this book, is unlike any other book, not just a collection of stories, or ideas, but a sacred text, a living text, constantly changing based on the eyes and the heart of the reader.

The very mystery of the text, becoming like water, means the words are fluid in their meaning, and their nature, changing to the times they are in, hence the scripture always being relevant to the surrounding culture. Although the ancient nature of the text remains, the application of the truths inside remains relevant, and important to all disciples of Christianity today.

Without sacred scripture, there can be no standard of truth, although we all argue, interpret, and wrestle with the meaning, the baseline meaning is apparent, Jesus Christ is Lord.

There has been textual criticism, and lots of study based on the different manuscripts of the bible, the different apparent errors, and paradoxes, the truth remains inside the text, hidden behind the words, it remains the person of Christ Jesus, the Word becoming flesh.

Christians all over the world understand the bible as the divine word of God, intersecting with humanity in history, and know that, as the ages of history pass, the study, praying and human thought on these holy verses remain.

The Bible has probably been one of the only works in history, that has attracted some of the best minds that have lived, and still do, to spend an inordinate amount of time, energy, and focus, to sift out the hidden messages, the complete interpretation.

The work remains a labor of love, embarked upon by the scholar, the academic and the devout, locked into the hours of daily study, we all sit before the pages, and find the words of God are also a very real visceral sound in our ears, not just speaking about meaning, but communicating relationship.

Every person reading the scriptures finds unique meaning in them. When reading the bible, the meaning changes not only from each other's reading of the word, but also as we mature in our understanding and revelation. The apparent literal meaning might be static in interpretation, but the practice teaches us to become more allegorical and metaphorical in our reading.

LECTIO DIVINA

The practice of Lectio Divina, explores this process of reading scripture, as a spiritual act, thinking, and pondering these divine words, as a path of discovery towards the spiritual life.

Due to the many layers of hidden meaning in these scriptures, the act of reading them while we live life, allows us to grow with the words, interpreting them, and then re-interpreting them as our perspective matures. In some sense the scriptures read us, we don't read them.

Scriptural reading as prayer goal, implies we are not reading to understand only, but also reading to hear, reading to listen to the voice of God behind the words.

The path of Lectio Divina is a deeply personal journey, you will need to bring your life to the practice; the private life that only you know about, and allow God, with an open heart, to guide you. Allowing His voice to speak to you, about your own problems, your own thoughts and ideas. The path of change that follows, can lead you to spiritual growth towards God.

Answering the why of "Lectio Divina" is clear: we do the practice, not for the sake of intellectual pursuit, but because to us, scripture is also a sacrament. The very act of encountering the words, is spiritual practice, spiritual work, just like praying, worshiping or any other spiritual pursuit of humanity.

Let us use an illustration — We and God are like two trees in a garden, planted apart, slowly growing towards each other as the years go by. The progress might seem unseen, slow, almost unnoticed by the passer by, yet steady progress is made with the constant growth.

Then one day, when the storms of life blow the leaves of your tree, you will find God's branches holding you up in the wind, and growing right next to you, the canopy of His love, His leaves healing your wounds.

THE PRACTICE OF LECTIO DIVINA

Before we start practicing, we need to understand the goal of the practice is to hear God's voice through scripture.

We often become to analytical and theological when reading the scripture. The bible is the "living word"; allow the sacred words to become alive to you, to speak to you, allow the scripture to read you.

This is not a one-way process, as with most other literature, you are now about to engage with the best-selling book in human history. A divine reading of scripture is then undertaken not as an act of study, but as an act of encountering the divine God while reading His words to humanity throughout the ages.

- **"Lectio" – Reading**
  The first step is to find a scripture to read. This can be any scripture you enjoy; the psalms are normally the best place to start but choose some scriptures you are familiar with to practice.

While you are reading, calm your heart and mind. Do not force on the practice, but allow the scripture to jump out at you, or see if there are any words that seem to catch your attention.

- **"Meditatio" – Reflection**

Re-read the scripture, with the focus on the parts where you felt God speaking to you, or the nudge of the Holy Spirit as you read the scriptures.

Reflect on what you believe God is saying to you, think about the scripture more deeply, and ask God to make His focus clear to you, so you can understand what He is saying.

Remember the Holy Spirit is there with you, helping you comprehend the divine reality.

- **"Oratio" – Respond**

After now reading the scripture for a third time, make sure you have a journal, and write down some of the ideas, and thoughts you learned from the passage. Most of us cannot remember the lessons the following day, so writing helps with the retaining process.

While you are writing take time to pray over the scripture, ask God questions, and write down some of the answers He gives you.

God does not mind brutally honest people; God can handle your humanity.

- **"Contemplatio" – Rest**

Sit silently and quietly ask God to finish the work He started within your heart, and in your being. You are a spiritual being, so take 10 minutes, and just allow your mind to be in contemplation and rest.

When the mind wonders, do not get upset, just slowly return to the scripture passage, and ask God to ground the words and thoughts into your being.

A completed lesson with God means the scripture needs to become part of your nature, and for this to happen, we need the work of the Holy Spirit, while being at rest.

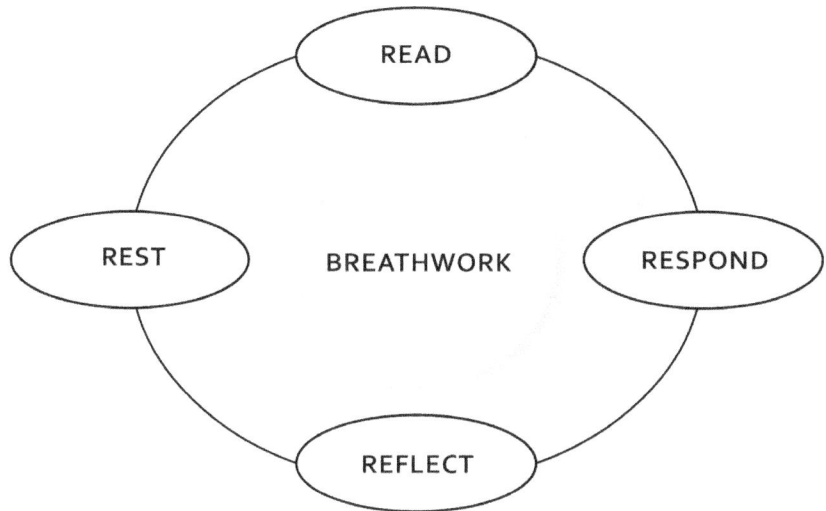

AN ALTERNATIVE APPROACH TO LECTIO DIVINA

Historically Lectio Divina has been cultivated with alternative approaches to the practice. Claire of Assisi developed her own method, which seems to be contrasted to her fellow Catholic Guigo the II, who developed a more rigid approach.

Clare of Assisi has a 4-pronged method which is quite different to the one prescribed in the normal traditional Lectio Divina.

Her Method can be described as follows:

- **"Intueri" – Gaze or Behold the Cross**
  In this action, the follower of Christ, gazes only at the cross, either externally by looking at the physical Icon, or more intently the focus of the interior gaze; the gaze of attention focusing on the crucified cross of Christ, indelibly etching the wounds of Jesus on our minds.

- **"Considerare" – Consideration**
  In this action one would consider the consequence of the cross, what is the hidden implications both personal and on a social and human species scale.

- **"Contemplari" – Contemplate**
  Allow the mind to contemplate, to consider, and in some sense,

allow the mind to focus on this reality.

The whole act of ruminating on the finished work of Jesus, the follower of Jesus can allow his mind to chew like a cow, allowing the sweet juices of the completed work to fill the whole being, while understanding, and meditating on this beloved sacrifice, and the heart of God allowing this to take place, what could the motivations of such a God be towards us.

Like a child, constantly rolling a new-found crystal in his hand, looking at all the different facets of the stone, and wondering in silence; allowing the awe and beauty to captivate the thoughts of the action of Christ, until the mind is completely enamored, and no bandwidth is allowed for other thoughts.

- **"Imitare" – Imitate**

The part of the practice that Clare of Assisi is also known for, her social justice, and her work for the poor and orphaned of society. The burden to all who see the sacrifice, to those who behold the lamb, they are bid to imitate, to become.

The Bible often bids the true disciples of Christ, not just to behold their God, but to become like Him, in their very actions, allowing the reality of their God, to influence and change the way they act.

A Christianity that is not linked to actions, is no faith at all.

Guigo II	Clare of Assisi
Read (*lectio*)	Gaze on the Cross (*intueri*)
Meditate (*meditatio*)	Consider (*considerare*)
Pray (*oratio*)	Contemplate (*contemplari*)
Contemplate (*contemplatio*)	Imitate (*imitare*)

(Armenian Cross)

VISIO DIVINA:

"divine seeing"

Visio Divina, as the name suggests "divine seeing," or in some sense recognizing in our seeing, the divine in the ordinary.

INFLUENCERS OF VISIO DIVINA

"Illiterate men can contemplate in the lines of a picture what they cannot learn by means of the written word."

– Pope Gregory I

St John of Damascus was born in 676, he was known as a polymath, with his studies in theology, law, philosophy, and music. He became a monk at Mar Saba in 706.

He wrote an important work called an "Apologetic Treatises against those Decrying the Holy Images" which was later used in 787 at the second council of Nicaea, to resolve the dispute against icons.

One of the famous quotes from the treatise is:

"How wise the Law is! How could one depict the invisible? How picture the inconceivable? How could one express the limitless, the immeasurable, the invisible? How give infinity a shape? How paint immortality? How put mystery in one place?"

He died in 749, at Mar Saba in Jerusalem, a Greek Orthodox monastery overlooking the Kidron valley.

Pope Gregory I, mentioned in the previous chapter, was also an advocate for Visio Divina. He had much influence in the Church.

VISIO DIVINA

Being sensitive, all my friends from various backgrounds, it is easy to look at this practice, and jump to idiolatry, or assume the practice of creating images is clearly a contravention of God's command to Israel not to create an image of God.

This quick assumption would be a grave error, and I would encourage you to delve a bit deeper into the practice, after all the same people we condemn, read the same bible we read, and come to a different conclusion.

Visio Divina is the practice of beholding and gazing at a sacred image until it inspires us to prayer and meditate on the divine.

While looking with alert awareness at the images, the creator of the image prays that God enlightens and awakens the viewer to sacred sacrament of divine desire of God, enflaming the divine passions within, and awaking the remembrance of the faithful towards the deeper realities.

When one gazes at the sacred, one is reminded: this world is not all there is, beyond this dream, a reality exists far deeper, and more eternal than our fleeting mundane routine.

Art and beauty have always carried these ethereal qualities, jolting the subconscious into an awakened state of recognizing the beauty in the ordinary. How many times do we visit an art gallery or look at some of the masters, and walk away from the experience, grateful to God for allowing us to be alive at this moment in history.

The subject matter of the sacred art, because of the intention of the artist, helps us to see the divine, and normally leads to silence, and a search for the deeper meaning of the art.

VISIO DIVINA AND THE ICON

An Icon is a sacred image used in religious devotion. Icons are used in various churches throughout history to depict the story of the bible and the people of the bible.

The Greek word "*eikon,*" is translated as "image" in the bible. This is not seen as an apparent misuse of the word because, when God created man in His divine image, God did not say Adam was an "idol."

The incarnation of Christ, the true icon (image) of God, which is the biggest argument for venerating icons, and yet not worshiping the physical object.

Jesus himself says, *"If you have seen me, you have seen the Father in heaven."*

When Adam fell, the temptation for Eve was, "you will be like God," however both Adam and Eve were created in the image of God already, hence the temptation was also one of identity.

The second Adam, Jesus, came to redeem the image of humanity, by taking on human flesh, by allowing divinity to indwell the image. Jesus then redeemed the very image of man, to once again be able to bear the image of God.

Jesus in this sense goes beyond the icon, Jesus becomes the incarnation of God, re-imaging the very nature of God in creation. The redemption of Christ is not just from sin, but the very identity of Man, He would say to them, *"I no longer call you servants but friends,"* thus changing the very relationship between God and man, to the original Adamic format.

We as new creation beings, can access the likeness and the image of God again, in our very human body, the resurrected body, is again accessible to those who would look beyond the now moment.

Does this mean we worship these images, and bring sacrifices to them? Surely not, and this should never be the case. The goal of the icon is to point to a far greater spiritual reality, you cannot depict God who is omnipresent, all powerful and immeasurable.

The infinite can never be limited in time and space, anything done in this material reality, only points to a far deeper truth hidden in plain sight. The icon is supposed to communicate truth, in visible symbolic form, but is never to be worshiped, or glorified beyond this point.

If you have been in a church, you would have seen all the drawings, all the pictures, all the images of the biblical stories, and wondered what the point is, some of the drawings seem quite frankly a bit badly done, like some amateur decided to try his hand at drawing the divine.

The fact of the matter is most others who have entered the church, have seen these icons as mere idols, an accusation leveled at the church, filled with idols, being worshiped by the faithful seeking physicality above spirituality.

This, however, is not the whole story, as we need to remember when these churches were created, well in most cases, most of the population could not read, or write, their only access to biblical stories are these very paintings we see every time we enter a building.

We do not condemn presentation slides, when we explain our preaching and teaching because for some reason our highly technological age has made it fine, the moment we paint some images on a wall, to explain a parable, now we are worshiping an idol, how do these ideas fit?

The Icon is theology in line and color, a visual depiction of theology, limited to the method of communication.

VISIO DIVINA AND ICONOGRAPHY

The definition for iconography is the visual images and symbols used in a work of art or in the study or interpretation of these.

This work of art is not open for interpretation like in modern art, the iconography carries strict rules and methods of creating the art.

Herewith some rules:

- **Light and Darkness**
  In normal art, light plays a more decorative role, however in spiritual art, the light and darkness take on spiritual capacity and meaning. God as the giver of light or surrounded in the dark cloud of uncreated light.

- **Faces and Movement/Gestures**
  Faces are supposed to express the spiritual character of the person, and the facial expressions are often there to create relationships between the characters.

- **Inverse Perspective**
  Sometimes the perspective is changed, almost making you feel like the person is coming to meet you, this is done to create the feeling of you being spiritually connected to the person in the icon.

- **Symbolism**

When the artist cannot express the spiritual meaning, they turn to symbols to assist with the process of conveying truth.

- **Silence and Stillness**
  There are very few icons where people are depicted as speaking, the lack of "noise" is supposed to convey a spiritual atmosphere and assist the viewer on meditating on the image and finding the hidden spiritual meaning.

ICONOGRAPHY VS ART

We understand that there were many quality artists in the middle ages, and through the history of the church, Iconography was really the practice of "sacred" art, or "theology in colors" with some very specific intentions and motivations.

The church wanted to communicate theological ideas, and thus, the process of creating art in churches had specific requirements and motivations. A priest or bishop would like to have certain areas of the church for contemplation, so the art they commissioned needed to communicate a specific spiritual atmosphere, and in other places another feeling needed to be conveyed.

The same does not apply to normal artist and masters of the middle ages, many of them incorporated their own interpretation of scriptures, their art, although depicting biblical scenes, included some other symbolic meaning, and other ideas the church, and Christianity does not necessarily agree with.

Although some of these artists created beautiful work, sometimes outside the sanction of the church, the intention and motivation behind the art is still communicated when gazing at the work. Be sure to check your own heart, and how certain images impact your ideas and thoughts.

We have become an over-visualized society, which means our sensitivity to images has been degraded, it takes time to retake the gates of our eyes, in the words of *Job 31:1 "I made a covenant with my eyes not to look lustfully at a young woman."* NIV

We need to understand that the images created in the church, mostly by painstakingly spending hours painting specific techniques and being very disciplined in how the art is created, this labor of love, sometimes by very faithful Christians in history, is what helps us to come to a place of consecration.

This might not be easy to replicate by simply viewing any digital image on your laptop or phone somewhere, due to the nature of the image, and the place of commissioning.

The icons we find at many churches were also created in an atmosphere of reverence and awe, this coupled with the atmosphere of silence and contemplation in most Orthodox churches, helps with the process of listening and hearing the voice of God.

Most priests and monks will not interrupt somebody weeping, or gazing intently at the icon, even frantically making notes while gazing intently at the icon, and trying to capture the divine voice, speaking to the Christian soul.

SIGNS AND SYMBOLS OF VISIO DIVINA

The whole bible is meant to be interpreted, most of the Book of Revelation is a complete book of signs and symbols, yet we do not stay there, and make our homes on the edifice of allegory and metaphor.

True Christian maturity sees the signs, the symbols, and is reminded of the spiritual truths they point towards. Understanding what the symbols mean, what rituals and rites point us towards, helps make our spiritual practice deeper, it moves us away from the mundane.

THE PRACTICE OF VISIO DIVINA

Icons reveal that there is no separation between the sacred and secular, everything in creation is sacramental, and speaks of the creator God, who created creation as a vehicle to communicate the spiritual realities. As some might express this reality, "as above, so below," earth is a dim reflection of the heavenly realities when viewed in the sacred light of revelation, from the perspective of Christ.

Find a church that you can spend some time in while practicing Visio Divina. Below is a process to allow the practice of Visio Divina to become part of your contemplative lifestyle. As you become familiar with this process, you will become freer to create your own process or method to experience God through Visio Divina.

- **Relax**

    Ask God to speak to you, and help you clearly understand His voice; allow your whole being to become part of the practice, your analytical soul, your intuitive soul, and your emotional soul.

- **Gaze with Focus**

    Gaze at the image, let your eyes rest on the characters, and objects in the image. Pay close attention to your emotions, as you look at parts of the image, and encapsulate the whole of the image in your gaze.

- **Read or Listen**

    Read or listen to portions of scripture that relate to the image before you, allow your own insights or ideas to come into focus. Remain receptive, with an open heart towards God to speak to you or reveal something personal to you.

    Release preconceived ideas you had about the image and allow an atmosphere of wonder and awe to fill your heart, as you ponder the Lord.

- **Re-gaze and Imagine**

    Gaze at the image again; now imagine yourself as part of the image, or as part of the scene taking place before you. What do you see, hear, taste or smell, engage your 5 senses, while you imagine yourself there? What is God inviting you to experience or understand as you become part of the image.

- **Personalization**

    Ask the Holy Spirit to guide you in this process. How do you now see the image or scene differently than before? Does the image invoke feeling of desire or spiritual hunger towards God, and what is the response God is asking you to have in this moment?

    Should you express something like forgiveness, gratitude, confession of sins, or praise and wonder at His divine goodness? How is the sacred presence of God embodied in this moment to you personally?

- **Incarnation**

    How does this "Visio Divina" impact your life today, right now, and in which areas of your life can you live Christ today towards others. What is Jesus saying to you personally today.

- **Retention**

    What about today's experience can you take away with you, and would you like to remember throughout the day and the week?

    Write down some thoughts now if you can find some time and space. Even though the thoughts and ideas sound simple and familiar, you are trying to capture the moment, and the feeling, do not judge what you journal, just write down what you feel you want to remember, or think upon later.

    Thank God for speaking to you in this moment, allowing you to hear His voice, through your eyes.

MY "VISIO DIVINA" TESTIMONY

While traveling to Bulgaria to visit some friends, and quite frankly trying to escape my life at that stage in early 2005, I was at a crossroad, I resigned from my work, and did not know what my next move should be.

My friends not being very spiritual, showed me some old churches and cathedrals of the town, as a tourist, I really enjoyed the old-world feeling of the buildings, and the spiritual atmosphere inside.

One day, I felt like going to town on my own, as the Easter Orthodox churches had their own charm, and I wanted to experience this on my own.

I sat down slowly in the corner of one monastery, silently gazing at the parable, I knew the biblical story well, and contemplated the parable while looking at the pictures. Suddenly I imagined how many people in the town, would do the same, many illiterate generations before me, sat here, looking at these walls, and hearing the priest explain the bible to them, learning about the goodness, and love of Jesus, from these beautiful walls.

Having converted back to Christianity from a few floundering years in Buddhism, my training taught me to observe, question, and remain non-judgmental at first, before making up my mind.

My protestant past tried to convince me to judge these churches, and judge these people, as mere idol worshipers, bowing before dead statues, and worshiping material things, and relics, instead of the one true God, Jesus Christ.

I had the option to become offended at their expression of Christianity, and yet, in this silent moment, with the priest chanting in the background, and reciting the morning vespers, I sat there, weeping, the words of the bible stories becoming more alive to me, than in all the years of theological study.

Quite clearly, I heard the voice of the Holy Spirit, "*son, it's time to come back home in a deeper way, not just knowing the truth, not just worshiping the right God, but actually becoming a person incarnating the truth to the people around you. Being a Christian and acting like Christ is not the same thing my son.*"

The words offended my sensibilities, these images like wolves, ripped away my religion, my fancy well-rehearsed excuses for not loving people, and in this moment, and till today, every time I enter a more conservative branch of Christianity, I remember this day, the day where Jesus challenged me to become the "incarnation," not just preach the message of incarnation.

Sometimes our misconceptions and preconceived ideas of symbols and icons with our Western attachment to their meaning, leave us impoverished of the richness of the word of God, in art form. We are quick to accept prophetic art and see meaning in it. Can we also turn our gaze on the icons of old to impact and enrich our experience of God? I pray we allow those icons to lead us deeper into God.

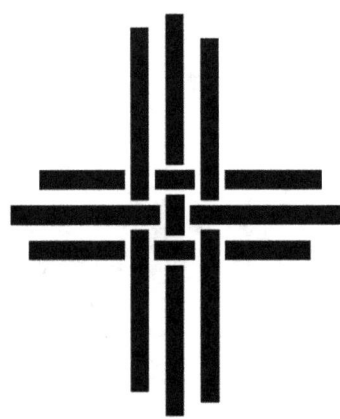

(St Michaels Cross)

SILENCE AND SOLITUDE

Pope Benedict XVI: "Silence has the capacity to open a space in our inner being, a space in which God can dwell, which can ensure that his Word remains with us, and love for him is rooted in our minds and hearts and animates our lives."

INFLUENCERS OF SILENCE AND SOLITUDE

Evagrius Ponticus is one of our most influential theologians and writers about silence in the Christian church, also one of the earliest. He was born in 345 in Turkey to a Christian family.

He was educated in Niksar and became a lector under Basil the Great. He later went to Constantinople where Gregory the Theologian made him a deacon. He then became the archdeacon.

After some character challenges, Evargius travelled to Jerusalem and became a monk. Although he did not stay there for a long time, it brought a lot of change in his life. He then travelled to Egypt and spent the remaining years of his life in Nitria and Kellia.

He was a great influencer to many church leaders and had many well-known students. He wrote a great deal of literature that impacted the church.

Evagrius Ponticus, De Oratione

"*By praying with perseverance and hope in the help of the divine grace the monk is led to that condition of mental stability (κατάστασις) which Evagrius identifies with the state of perpetual freedom from passions or apatheia. However, differently from what a modern reader could think, for Evagrius apatheia is not a condition of mere indifference or carelessness, but what kindles in the intellect a profound love for God, which leads it to transcend the sensible dimension and reach perfect communion with Him."*

We understand then that the place one needs to reach to achieve the "mental stability," is achieved in some by the practice of silence and solitude, amongst the many other practices he suggests.

Nilus of Sinai born in the late 4th Century, was also one of the earlier proponents of silence and solitude.

He was an officer at the court of Constantinople, we do not know much about his birth or his life in childhood. He was a great supporter of St John of Chrysostom and denounced many of his detractors.

In 404 he took his son, and left his wife, and their other son, to join a monastery at Mount Sinai to be a monk. He was ordained by the bishop of Palestine Elusa. He served at Mount Sinai, after some adventures to find his son who was captured and sold as a slave, due to attacks on the monasteries by the Saracens.

Some of his key teachings about solitude and silence are as follows:

- Strive to render your mind deaf and dumb during prayer; then you will be able to pray as you ought.

- When you pray as you ought, there may come into your mind things about which it seems right to be angry with your brother. There is absolutely no anger against your brother which could be justified.

- Do not pray that things may be according to your desires, for they are not always in keeping with the will of God. Better pray as you were taught, saying: "Thy will be done."

- Strive not to pray against someone in your prayer, lest you destroy what you are building, by making your prayer an abomination (before God).

Although he teaches many more things about prayer, these key thoughts should assist us in our search for God using silence and solitude as our method.

There are many church fathers who wrote about the ascetic life, separating yourself from the world you live in, although I believe most of us are either unable to live this life, or choose to disagree with the ascetic path, what one finds valuable in these teachings is the value and need for solitude.

In a world where silence and solitude seem hard to find, and even harder to desire, I believe we should not judge the church fathers who lived ascetic lives, disagreeing with their lifestyle, but rather understand these practices as available to those who would seek momentary solitude in their daily lives.

A value for time alone is something we can all develop, not just time spent being alone, but time with God, time without all the entertainment culture we so desire. The inner life can only be cultivated in the gardens of silence and solitude, where the heart, and mind, filled with God become great places of fruitful contemplation.

TYRANNY OF NOISE

We live in a world of noise, the hustle and bustle from early morning "get ready," to late evening "just one more episode." The towns and cities we once knew become cities and metropolitan areas, and large tracts of land become urbanized at a rate never seen before in the history of humanity.

Everything is changing, and everything is becoming noisier; the constantly growing population, already at 8 billion people, the earth is becoming a very noisy place.

We all live in this place of noise, we will our lives with sounds, that is how we have become accustomed to experiencing the world, from Bluetooth headsets to entertainment systems, our existence creates a systematic need to build sound and frequency into our lives.

We become more absorbed in this ocean of noise, our inner reality fades slowly into the waves of sound, that surround and engulf us.

What then shall we do to escape the tyranny of noise, how shall we create space, and silence in the future?

VALUE OF SILENCE

We, for the most part, enjoy our busy, noisy lives. We enjoy the sounds that surrounds us and the comfort it gives us as we do not want to be alone. The question then becomes even more pertinent to answer: why is silence valuable, why is the lack of sound so important to the development of the inner man?

Silence is in fact the natural state of man. If you sit silently on a sofa at home, your very original state is silence, before any sound, noise or vibration exists, silence must be the starting point when engaging human life.

This is the very nature of creation, when God spoke, "let there be...,", he spoke from a place of silence, God created from silence, the very act of God "speaking" means that God initiated sound from a place of complete and utter vibrationless existence; some would call this "ex Nelio" creation from nothing.

It follows that every act of creation from this divine act of creation shall be best started from a place of silence, not the silence of chaos, or the place of nothing, but an inner silence created by the individual to be in this place of complete rest, and inner peace and silence, enabling creative flow and impulse on a sustainable level.

The cultivation of silence, as truly an act of spiritual hunger, the silent man realizes all answers, thoughts and ideas have come to an end. All the possible variable ideas have reached their conclusion, only one thing remains, in this divine act of surrender, silence is birthed in the human heart.

This silence of humility builds teachable hearts, able to receive the correction from God, not as an emotional or intellectual rebuke, but as the loving movement of God's hand, speaking into the heart of the child, encouraging other areas of exploration and growth.

Our apparent suspicion of God's goodness, and God's commitment to stay intimately involved in the affairs of man, always creates an inner tension in this place of silence.

We have become so offended with God's invisible nature, His well-hidden hand behind the scenes of our lives, slowly moving us to awakening. This apparent absence creates within us a complete loss of words, a feeling of abandonment, as circumstances seems to crush our comprehension of divine goodness.

The mystic, however, learns that every step in this place of apparent absence and abandonment, is a place of incubation, moving beyond the senses, and circumstances. Every movement of the mystic is a movement of growth, exploration, not of the outer reality, but the inner trust, coming to a knowing that the God of heaven, and earth, is also the God of me.

THE ART OF LISTENING

Why do we remain silent when someone talks? The reason is so "elementary"; we wish to listen, we are focused on the sound and the frequency emitted from the person, and therefore delving into the meaning of their words, and their communication verbal or otherwise.

The art of listening is then not just an obsession with focus on sound, or an effort to listen for the sake of hearing within the noise of life or trying to find meaning within sound.

The true art of listening leans more towards the subtitle movement of intention, the slow movement of body language, the feeling the sounds create the coming together of the sound, and then deciphering the meaning.

In some sense those embarking on the path of silence, become masters of interpretation, looking beyond the surface meaning. Symbolism, signs, and other patterns of recognition then evolve into the conversation with silence, where the true treasure is found, amid the meander into meaning.

The maps of meaning, the adventure of understanding, and comprehending the hidden, apprehending the undercurrent of sounds, and then building a systematic grid for spiritual secrets.

When we engage with silence as a practice of divine encounter, listening is highlighted in the absence of sound. We should not listen with the intention to reply, or the thought of building meaning or interpreting before the divine sentence is complete; when the full stop ends the sentence of the Godly utterance, our hearts, minds, and spirits intermingle, to then realize the meaning. Sometimes, this meaning is built over time, based on life experiences.

The art of listening is an art due to the level of patience and skill required, most good art takes time, so does this art. Time needs to pass, the slow-moving of reality needs to progress before the art can be learned and practiced.

SILENCE AS A VALUE IN COMMUNITY

It might surprise you to know, but not all silence is created as equal. The moment we start building places of silence and quiet peace, we start learning that not all silence is healthy, and not all silence cultivates the same results in our lives.

We all know the uncomfortable silences in conversations, or in meeting strangers, or the silences that makes your hair stand on end. These silent pauses in our lives, builds a feeling of dis-ease, and does not bring us to a place of reflection.

The intention of silence is important, when building a community of silence, a community of reflection where silence is celebrated, we also need to allow the silence to help people discover the value of this community.

We cannot create closed systems of silence, where the outsider always feels like an outsider because the silence strangles community, conversation, and friendship.

Silence should be cultivated, like a sensitive orchid, slowly allowing the water of love, to filter into the moments of silence, and coaching, training, and building communal silence that elevates awareness, and consciousness.

SOLITUDE IS NOT LONELINESS

Let us now shift our attention to solitude and the importance of the practice of solitude within our lives.

Solitude is self-imposed aloneness, a state of isolation, and can even be viewed as "set-apart." The purpose of solitude and silence for that matter, should be for the edifying of the soul. Creating a space within ourselves to hear God, to become aware of blind spots that need attending within our lives, and to find our spiritual rhythm again. When we look at the life of Jesus, He frequently isolated himself in solitude to engage with the Father.

Now in the morning, having risen a long while before daylight, He went out and departed to a solitary place, and there He prayed.

Mark 1:35

And when he had sent the multitudes away, he went up into a mountain apart to pray: and when the evening was

> *come, he was there alone.*
> **Matthew 14:23**

Loneliness on the other hand, is imposed by external situations, or internal isolation. Wikipedia describes loneliness as an unpleasant emotional response to perceived isolation.

Many in our generation experience loneliness at some point in their lives. It is a natural occurrence as we go through the ebbs and flows of life. But loneliness could become your permanent state of being. In that instance, it is so important to reach out and resolve the matter.

Life can sometimes be cruel beyond words and if you feel isolated, or completely alone, without any ability to connect around you, I would like to encourage you, find the poor and destitute around you, and give them something, build a practice of blessing the poor, and soon, those alone moments will disappear, as something inside starts changing, your external reality will change.

Choosing solitude as a practice can be challenging, but also extremely rewarding; the reason, purpose and motivation should, however, be clear as to combat any negative thoughts during a time set apart for solitude.

SOLITUDE AND THE DEVELOPMENT OF ASCETICISM

Part of this lifestyle of silence, becomes the practice of Ascetism, although this is practiced in both the eastern orthodox church, and the catholic church, the practice started with the desert fathers, with their desire to dedicate themselves to the seeking of God.

Asceticism can be described as "severe self-discipline and avoiding of all forms of indulgence, typically for religious reasons" as per the Oxford dictionary. We will look at the role of solitude in this practice, although it is for the purpose of reference and to reinforce the importance of solitude.

The early church was persecuted by the Roman empire, The Syrian and Armenian early church, then moved into seclusion to focus on their spiritual development. Adversity creates the greatest motivator for pursuing the things that we are persecuted for. This persecution ignited the fire within the early church to press even harder for a meaningful relationship with God.

Some of them becoming hermits, dedicating their time and effort to the pursuit of God in complete isolation and solitude.

Although this lifestyle of silence and solitude permeated the culture, the desert soon became too small to hide the glorious souls of these men and women, and communities would be attracted to them, and form around them to seek spiritual guidance and tuition.

Lunacy serves no divine purpose. Remember; the aim of solitude is to find the friendship of God, to commune with the divine, and create a that space where humanity can encounter God in a way that uniquely prioritizes not just the persona of God, but also focuses time and space of the clarification of desire. Housing a space on earth, where the temple inside the human heart can be tended to with the complete attention of the one whom would wait in silence, praying for hours, and focus their intention, and desire on one true outcome, the pleasure and company of God's very nature.

WHEN SILENCE AND SOLITUDE BECOMES PUNISHMENT

We have all heard the phrase "to give somebody the silent treatment" or put children in the "naughty corner." As a society, we have created punishment around silence and solitude. Practices that are in fact, very gentle and focused on love.

We use our silence to punish people, to demean their words, to build a fortress of quiet resentment. Solitude is used to isolate people and through our actions, we "ex-communicate" people to a life of solitude.

This is one of the most painful methods or "spiritual technology" that we can use to put our friends and family in solitary silent confinement.

This is not the silence any of us want to be faced with, a silence of absence, where the voice of a friend or family member is silenced and creates distance between people. These methods of passive violence threaten the nature of silence, and builds fear, and loneliness.

We never want to create a space where silence is used to build walls of disconnection and buttress our lack of compassion and humanity away from the words of life, that Christ communicates to the world through our lives.

Solitary confinement was practiced in various war times, to get information via this extreme form of torture, creating an atmosphere for delusion and hallucination. The same also happens in prisons to a lesser extent, where solitary confinement is used as punishment under certain circumstances.

We are not in a war with each other, we are in community. These forms of punishment should be removed from our society and we need to mature into a people that can talk about the differences that we have. We need to learn to love each other and allow the beauty of silence to be the "places within the music,", to be the comforting pause in conversation. Solitude should be a posture we choose to submit to, for the benefit of the soul and the deepening of our relationship with God.

When any person looking to "self-isolate" themselves or commit themselves to the process of solitude, they need to be prepared for this journey. The preparation for solitude is often the lessons learned by the generation before, in how to avoid delusion, and build intimacy with God.

The communities around the desert fathers and mothers developed a certain preparative way, with sayings, exercises and practical advice for the hermit or ascetic person.

Lunacy serves no divine purpose; the aim of solitude is to find the friendship of God.

THE PRACTICE OF SILENCE AND SOLITUDE

The practice of silence and solitude is a personal journey. One of choosing to set aside the time to pursue silence, to pursue solitude. This is a practice going against the grain of society as we love our busy sound-filled lives.

Quietly sit, and listen, make sure you are surrounded by silence – no, you do not need to go somewhere; just try to be in a place that is silent or quiet, maybe you will need to do this before bedtime.

As you sit, listen, do not just hear the noise of your life, really listen, and list the number of things you can hear, the noise around you.

Ok now that you have catalogued the noise, let's time the silence. This will help you to feel that there is a limit to the time spent and help our minds to feel we are not wasting time. Set your stopwatch on your phone for 5 min and tell yourself you can spoil yourself today with 5 minutes of silence.

Sit, listen, and see if you can hear sounds beyond the noise, if you can hear birds, how many if you can hear cars, what type of cars, and what is below the noise of the cars?

As you unpeel the noise, you will hear the layers of sound, and yes, if you can get some noise-canceling headphones, you could then go beyond the noise, and listen. Just listen, as you hear the silence, just enjoy the soundless existence.

And if you really feel adventurous today, try to imagine life before life existed, what would space have sounded like, before God said, "Let there Be...," before the Divine sound, before the "noise" of creation. What is the silence then? In this moment, just imagine with me, you are with God the Father, and like old friends, you do not say anything in this moment.

You are giving God, "a moment of silence" before He speaks the first words ever spoken in creation. You can be, in this sacred silence, this immortal, eternal, timeless moment, where Christ was slain before the creation of the creation, in this moment, you are able to be, at least in your imagination, sharing the sacred moment with God, before it all happened as we heard it did.

A story is told as much by silence as by speech.
Susan Griffin

(Shamrock Cross)

MINDFULNESS

Mindfulness is a mental state obtained through focusing one's awareness or consciousness on the present moment; calmly acknowledging and accepting one's feelings, thoughts, and physical sensations.

INFLUENCERS OF MINDFULNESS

"May we be faithful to observe our own lives, be humble enough to admit our sins, and resilient enough to let God realign us toward his purposes."

— Holly Sprink

Francisco de Osuna was born in 1492, in Osuna, Seville, Spain. He entered the military and was part of the conquest of Tripoli on the 25th of August 1510, but he chose to enter the life of the church, and studied at the University of Seville, where he focused on Latin and Rhetoric as his major subjects.

After having made a pilgrimage to Santiago de Compostela and experiencing an epiphany, he completed his studies in 1513 at the age of 21. He then took the habit of the church, in the Order of Friars Minor, in the province of Castile, the founder of the order being Francis of Assisi.

He then studied at the House of Philosophy in Torrelaguna from 1514 to 1518, where he also took the vows of the order. He completed his studies in philosophy focusing on the 3 major themes of the time, Scotism, Scholasticism and Nominalism.

In 1523 Francisco entered a retreat house, Salceda, situated near Guadalajara, this allowed him to build a practice of solitude where he could spend at least a few weeks in solitude focusing on prayer and meditation.

In 1537 he returned to Spain, where he wrote his final work the "The Third Spiritual Alphabet." It was begun at Salceda, finished at Escalona, and was first published in Toledo in 1527.

Although his writings do not only focus on Meditation; his works had a huge effect on Teresa of Avila and impacted her whole way of understanding prayer. Francisco developed the "way of recollection" or "the narrow gate," which was later explained and expounded on by Teresa.

The other two major concepts which he first focused on were that prayer and recollection should be done "without ceasing"; our daily lives and chores should in no way be separated from our times of focused prayer. The "Holy Habit,", of continuous focus, which in some way can be described as constant mindful awareness, or just living with a constant awareness of divine presence, without the need to create an artificial divide between sacred and secular space in our lives.

Francisco also focused on learning to quiet the soul, and the faculties, to listen to the voice of the master who speaks "the language of silence." One of the major themes in the "Third Spiritual Alphabet" is "recollection as a cure of the distracted mind."

Teresa of Avila read his work in her youth, and this greatly impacted her, and the path she followed for the rest of her life. In some way, one could describe Francisco a spiritual mentor. Theresa writes the following:

"My uncle gave me a book. It is called The Third Spiritual Alphabet and endeavors to teach the prayer of recollection. And although during this first year I read many good books, I did not know how to proceed in prayer or how to be recollected. And so I was very happy with this book and resolved to follow that path with all my strength. I began to take time out for solitude, to confess frequently and to follow that path, taking the book for my master (Life, p67)."

Jon Kabat Zinn was born in 1944 in New York. After his graduation, he studied at MIT and completed his Ph.D. in molecular biology in 1971. While at MIT he started his ideas about the effect of meditation on the human psychology.

He studied under many Buddhist and Zen masters, and then adapted their techniques to the Western mind, removing the Eastern ideas, and concepts linked to Buddhist philosophy. What remained was an 8-week course in mindfulness, called Mindfulness-Based Stress Reduction.

In 1991 he published his book, "Full Catastrophe Living: Using the

Wisdom of Your Body and Mind to Face Stress, Pain, and Illness," outlining his ideas on meditation, and detailed instruction regarding his practice, which was developed outside organized religion.

His work prefers the scientific effects of the practice on the human mind, to deal with stressors and trauma based on recognized scientific method, instead of just hoping things work.

The work done by this movement in the USA focused on the proven effects of the method he developed to assist with anxiety, depression, and other measurable, quantifiable medical-tested diseases.

> *Men's hearts failing them for fear, and for looking after those things which are coming on the earth: for the powers of heaven shall be shaken. KJV*
> **Luke 21:26**

MINDFULNESS

What I appreciate about the mindfulness movement, is that they have stripped out all the spiritual stuff, developed techniques, and then tested these techniques in a medical setting, and showed repeatable results, based on these systems.

The bible mentions the word meditation 20 times, in the context of scripture, and the practice of our faith, however, in modern terms, some Christians feel uncomfortable with the Eastern tags and labels placed on this practice.

Some of their concerns are justified, and hence, I endeavor to only mention and discuss the mindfulness practice as a scientifically tested practice for those reading this book and wanting something with more scientifically substantiating evidence of change.

We will also review how mindfulness has its place within Christian contemplation and how we can approach the subject.

As a side note: Our faith is actually "Eastern" not "Western." Judeo-Christian practice and development have always been eastern, the "Middle East" is just a concept developed by us, to somehow bring separation between our two worlds. Europe has always been part of the west, and Israel part of the east. The Christian desire to look to the east for new answers, is simply like a child, longing to go home, and find some answers that were lost at the beginning of the journey.

Our modern world focuses on the future and has all kinds of self-help methods to develop our goals, discover our destiny and purpose on earth. In an age lost without meaning, we are trying to find this meaning in the future, we have less value for the past, and even lesser value for the now.

This practice focuses on the now, or the "eternal now" as some would suggest. I know this is very counter intuitive to some, but in reality, we only have this moment. We need to learn to live in moments, the future then comes into the context of a thousand moments stacked into a framework and way of being.

We have more chance of achieving our goals, if we learn to live incremental lives, appreciating every moment. What would be the point of achieving a goal, but then realizing you cannot remember the journey of how you got where you are today.

The mechanisms of mindfulness will be focusing on breath, and things like learning to eat with awareness, and then using our awareness to practice certain techniques. Discovering how becoming more sensitive to our senses, can lead to more consciousness of the reality around us, which then helps us to become more sensitive to every reality of God in life.

Like any journey in life, mindfulness provides us with some obstacles we will need to overcome. Learning to live and appreciate our body and listening to our body might be uncomfortable at first.

We will also learn to pay attention to our walking and body posture habits, some of these habits are not healthy, so change will be a necessary result.

The way we speak, and the words we use, will become part of this journey of change.

As we become more aware of our habits, patterns, and ways of being, the process of change can lead us toward wonderful discoveries about ourselves.

The desire to change can then cause a huge shift in our body language, self-confidence, and overall change in the way we live life, the people we attract, and the overall quality of life.

Discovery of the beauty and special qualities we were created with, is a great process to help us walk in gratitude, change our attitude towards life, and everything else.

MINDFULNESS IN CHRISTIANITY

Why then do we explore this practice, if originated in the East, it is clearly based on another faith.

The fact remains that mindfulness techniques are common to man, not just certain faith groups.

We understand this practice to be re-introduced to the West via the mindfulness movement, however, this same practice was used by the desert fathers and mothers of Egypt and Syria.

There are also lesser-known roots in the Celtic tradition called "rinnfheitheamh," which could be translated as "the edge of waiting" or "waiting at the edge."

In 1975 John Main started bringing the idea of "Christian Meditation" back into use and assisting main line Christians to access this ancient path of prayer through Christ.

Although a figure with a colored past, John deliciated his life to the Benedictine order, and after much opposition to his work and effort to establish a meditation center in Ealing Abbey, in the UK, he and Laurence Freeman, left to establish a Benedictine monastery in Montreal, Quebec, which was focused on meditation and mindfulness.

John was greatly influenced by Thomas Merton, and the community he was able to establish at Abbey of Our Lady of Gethsemane, in Kentucky USA, based on contemplation and meditation.

This place inspired him to start his own community which then flourished into the monastic community in Montreal Canada.

John died in 1982, and his partner and friend Laurence Freeman, continued the work of setting up meditation centers globally now called the "World Community for Christian Meditation," hosting meetings and teaching the practice based on the teaching of John Main.

Mindfulness in Christianity is a practice that fits well within the contemplative lifestyle and when one engages in the practice of mindfulness with the intent of — a deeper, more meaningful relationship with God, the practice can become instrumental in changes — in areas of being that most people can appreciate a little help!

Mindfulness as an act of observing the now, is intricately connected in the Christian life, to gratitude and appreciation for the process of the practice. Mindfulness then helps to showcase the progress within the contemplative practice.

THE PRACTICE OF THE MIND

The idea of mindfulness then means one needs to start looking at the mind, understanding on a psychological way the mind works, and understand the physiological patterns of the mind.

The practice of mindful contemplation, sitting in silence, allowing the silence to permeate into the being, and not trying to think about nothing, but allowing this quiet place to permeate the moment of now.

This would then move into the practice of allowing all thoughts that come from the unconscious to surface into the consciousness, where the mind perceives their existence, but does not dwell on their reality, but rather allows them to fly away, like a little bird perching on the trees of ideas, and then being allowed to fly onwards.

Mindfulness then, is the practice of dealing with the thoughts, and ideas of the mind, or put another way, "being mindful" of what is in the mind.

As one observes the mind, and the thoughts, the challenge becomes not to judge the thoughts, or ideas, not to attach any meaning, or any thinking apparatus to the thoughts, but rather just allowing the thoughts to flow away, like water from a river.

A MISCONCEPTION ABOUT MEDITATION

Because mindfulness is linked to meditation, we need to review a misconception about meditation to avoid falling into a trap; thinking that we cannot do meditation or mindfulness.

Many people in the protestant movement have attacked the whole idea of allowing the mind to become empty, because an unsubstantiated fear exists of the devil jumping into the head and stay lodged there.

The question then becomes: "Where is this "open space" that the devil can jump into when God filled you with the Holy Spirit, and surrounded your whole soul with His divine light, when you became a Christian or converted to Christianity?"

We must believe that the divine light of God allowed into the heart and mind of the believer once conversion takes place from any belief system into Christianity, should then be able to dwell in the temple of that believer, and not allow any other being or entity to enter, unless by the free choice and will of the believer.

As believers in Jesus Christ, we know God's light is stronger than the darkness of this world, some would argue that darkness can still linger, and that would be accurate. However, demonic oppression and possession is not the same thing, and both require some level of co-operation and willful agreement by the believer.

The process of mindful contemplation is exactly this, removing all the shards of humanity, and uncovering the untrue hidden thoughts and ideas, motivations and lies we have told ourselves for many years.

When we talk about deliverance in the church, both catholic and protestant, the media has had more influence on the thinking of the Christian, than the bible or the true dogma of the church. We cannot believe that Christians are able to be infected by this pandemic of evil as if they are now the playground of the evil one. What would the point be of Christian conversion, if the same Christian then becomes completely at the mercy of the one he is being converted from.

We have made the demonic realms, and the evil atmosphere of this world so powerful in our perceived reality that our hearts and minds forget that many of the things we are currently worried about, the very fear we believe in, are based on the evil one, convincing us, we serve a God who is somehow less God than what the bible says.

Few Christians acknowledge that once a person converts from another faith into Christianity, a specific angel is created by God, to guard and help this person along their path of maturity. Whether Catholic or protestant, the angel does not know the difference, the angel of God, sees the desire for Jesus in the heart of man, sees the choice to become a follower of Jesus, and then is allowed to guard this choice, until this person dies, or chooses another way, which is not Christ Jesus and Him crucified.

No good father on earth welcomes a child into his house, and does not assign helpers and workers, to bring this child in his house to a place of maturity, yet somehow, we believe God in heaven, the very Father of Lights, is somehow a Father neglecting to protect those who put their hearts into His hands.

MINDFULNESS AND HEARTFULNESS

Since the middle ages man has always viewed the brain as our "core thinking capacity." This idea has been challenged by many new discoveries in medicine looking at all the thinking and cognitive systems in the body.

Although this is not a scientific book, and we are not exploring the realms of neurology, the current discoveries of the link between the mind and the heart are becoming clearer as our science develops better methods of testing.

> *For as he thinks in his heart, so is he. "Eat and drink!" he says to you, but his heart is not with you...*
> **Proverbs 23:7**

This verse clearly states there is cognitive activity happening in the heart, so the question now becomes, what do we mean by mindfulness, when we explore the idea that the heart is also thinking.

Scripture also clearly tells us to "guard your heart, because from it flows ...".

So, the act of mindful contemplation, can also then be exposed as "heartfulness," or being aware of what is happening in the heart. When we contemplate, and our thoughts enter the mind, what our mind is communicating is not just the busy thoughts of our intellect, but in fact, the very act of silencing the thoughts, also brings into view the feelings hidden in our hearts.

You will see this when attending a mindfulness course, or attending some classes on meditation, many people will experience emotional responses, and their emotional triggers start firing. This is because the silence and peace flooding into the mind is now reaching deeper into the subconscious levels or experience.

The heart and mind experience then leads to more understanding of our inner man, and our whole being starts aligning to the reality of self. When the heart and the thoughts of the heart are explored, the alignment of the thoughts of the heart, and the thoughts of the mind, starts creating a synergy of soul, which then builds and elevates the human identity, and the new "higher soul" dimension.

The process in terms of heart thinking is often more complex, one needs to give space for the feelings to emerge, allowing the feelings "about" something to give more guidance as to the thinking of the heart.

How about that "gut" feeling, or the ability to intuitively make judgement calls based only on the moment of peace one feels in the situation.

The research pertaining to this "heart-mind" connection is referred to as the microbiome–gut–brain axis. Intuition and thinking are being considered to reside in the relative proximity of the stomach and relates to how the brain is linked to the gut, and in my thinking the kidney and liver functions.

> *I the LORD search the heart, I try the reins, even to give every man according to his ways, and according to the fruit of his doings.*
> **Jeremiah 17:10 KJV**

In this verse the word "Reins," is translated, however, this word means kidneys, so in reality our whole body plays a part in our awareness and perception of the world. This chapter is not written to explain how the human body creates awareness and perception, but when we start looking at mindful work, we need to understand; some of the thoughts are not just happening in the mind, but the whole body is taking part in this practice.

It is important to note that, when we start with the contemplative path, a healthy body is required, not just for the sake of concentration and focus, but also for clarity. If the body is under pressure, or there are medical problems, one needs to be aware that the mindful practice is not a closed-circuit system.

Some teachers have alluded to this as an EQ (Emotional Quotient), which is more complex to explain, suffice to say, the complexity of emotions and feelings pertaining to spiritual development need much more attention, and one needs to start looking at the development of mindful contemplation in the context of heartful contemplation.

Mindfulness asks of us to view our thoughts, our bodies, our surroundings with an openness to understand where we are in our soul. This understanding brings correction to the areas that need attention, and in so doing a healthy soul environment is cultivated.

A healthy soul is a good place for the word of God to rest and the relational experience we have with the divine to change our being and bring us to a place where we can relate to the divine in purity and not through our own misgivings or perceptions.

Mindfulness as a practice is thus a means to an end within the Christian contemplative lifestyle. The end is the relationship we have with God, and the experience of His love for us.

THE PRACTICE OF MINDFULNESS

The practice of being mindful can by some be viewed as a continuous practice of being present and aware throughout the day. And this might be true. We will, however, look at a simplified practice of a mindfulness exercise.

- Sit in a relaxed posture — Close your eyes and connect with the sensations of your seated body.
- Take three long, deep, nourishing breaths — Breathing in through your nose and out through your mouth.
- Ask yourself:
    - What is my intention for today?
    - How might I have the best impact today?
    - What quality of mind do I want to develop?
    - How do I take care of myself?
    - During difficult situations, how might I be more compassionate to others and myself?
    - How will I feel more fulfilled?

- Set your intention clearly for the day ahead:
    o   For example, "Today, I will be ……."
- Check in with yourself during the course of the day.
- Pause, take a breath, and revisit your intention.
- Intentionality shifts the quality of your communications, relationships, and emotions.

Reflection is always a powerful way to end any contemplative practice and with mindfulness it is imperative to include reflection in the conclusion of your practice. Not only will you be able to gauge the progress of the practice, but your progress throughout your day.

(Japanese Cross)

DETACHMENT

CHAPTER 9

A state in which a person overcomes their attachment to desire for things, people or concepts of the world and thus attains a heightened perspective. (Wiki)

INFLUENCERS OF DETACHMENT

"If all images are detached from the soul, and it contemplates only the Simple One, then the soul's naked being finds the naked, formless being of the divine unity, which is there a being above being, accepting and reposing in itself. Ah, marvel of marvels how noble is that acceptance, when the soul's being can accept nothing else than the naked unity of God!" (Be Renewed in Your Spirit)

Meister Eckhart

When looking at detachment, in the West, we mostly link this to other belief systems outside of Christianity, and their view on the subject.

The two major leaders in the Christian faith when we look at detachment were John Climacus and Meister Eckhart.

Born in 579, in Syria, as described earlier in the book, John Climacus was a desert father, and wrote a book, "the ladder of divine ascent," where most of his ideas on detachment are captured.

When looking at the life of John and contemplating his thoughts on detachment based on his monastic and ascetic lifestyle, we assume his choice to live in isolation, then allowed him to renounce all his worldly cares, and worries, and easily progress from this renunciation, into a lifestyle of detachment.

Meister Eckhart, born in the 12th century, also wrote about detachment, and in some sense is the modern father of detachment in the Christian West. He writes about God in terms of "nothingness." Many scholars assume he is then moving beyond his theistic concept of a personal and trinitarian doctrine. Which is not the case.

What is absent in most of the scholarship is a lack of understanding about the extent to which the influence the Jewish philosopher Maimonides affected Meister Eckhart's ideas on nothingness.

The understanding of this concept is to be dissected as "no" — "thing" — "ness"; which in some respects is more a focus on non-materiality of divinity, and thus a focus on the "spiritual" nature of God, instead of a leaving behind of the Christian church, or the theology of the trinity.

Meister Eckhart understood the role of the intellect and its deceiving capability before quantum physics discovered the effect of the observer on the double-slit experiment. Meister Eckhart understood the metaphysical problem being presented, the very act of observing God, influences God, and the observer becomes the focal point of the problem.

The answer for Meister Eckhart lies in detachment, or "becoming poor and empty." He resolves the problem of ego by writing in his letters about the need to empty. He realizes the idolatry of his own misconceptions about God, is now becoming his greatest obstacle, and his solution to this is the "breakthrough" of being re-born in Christ, as part of the divine family, becoming in a sense part of the trinity, and able to supersede the human limitation of separation, and observation.

Becoming a partaker in the divine family resolves the crisis experienced by the onlooker, and removes nihilism from the equation, with emptiness remaining as a divine gift, enabling the human soul to comprehend nothingness by the lack of materiality.

DETACHMENT

Detachment is not as much a practice as it is simply a place of being, a state of being, however, one needs to know this place exists for it to be able to manifest in our lives.

The traditional impression of detachment speaks of the idea of a relationship between people. It is normally used in the context of the relationship man has with the world, and the people in it. In the context of the Christian understanding this detachment is not as much in relationality, but in the context of things, or materiality.

This detachment can be described in a biblical way; let us look at two verses.

> *If you were of the world, the world would love you as its own; but because you are not of the world, but I chose you out of the world, therefore the world hates you.*
>
> **John 15:19 ESV**

> *Beloved, I implore you as aliens and strangers and exiles [in this world] to abstain from the sensual urges (the evil desires, the passions of the flesh, your lower nature) that wage war against the soul.*
>
> **1 Peter 2:11 AMP**

When looking at biblical text, we understand this is not the gnostic way of putting less value in the world, we are here to make a difference, but instead not to let our emotions and our hearts be attached to worldly attractions.

Another way to describe detachment is the Ignatian way of indifference, as he suggests the concept "making use of those things that help to bring us closer to God and leaving aside those things that don't."

> *Do not love the world or the things in the world. If anyone loves the world, the love of the Father is not in him. For all that is in the world—the desires of the flesh and the desires of the eyes and pride of life[a]—is not from the Father but is from the world. And the world is passing away along with its desires, but whoever does the will of God abides forever.*
>
> **1 John 2:15-17 ESV**

We realize this relationship with the world we live in is a precarious relationship, we love the people in the earth, we endeavor to serve them, but we are not co-depending on the world, we do not derive our value, or our solace from this earth, our home and our heart are elsewhere.

When our affections are tempered by the fire of the fear of God, our hopes and our dreams change, the whole direction of our affection moves to a relationship with the divine, and then to manifest this relationship to those around us.

The centrifugal point of our existence is not just the ebbs and flows of live, and the affections of our circumstances, but the reality of our being founded in God.

> *Do not think that I came to bring peace on earth. I did not come to bring peace but a sword. For I have come to 'set[a] a man against his father, a daughter against her mother, and a daughter-in-law against her mother-in-law'; and 'a man's enemies will be those of his own household.' He who loves father or mother more than Me is not worthy of Me. And he who loves son or daughter more than Me is not worthy of Me. And he who does not take his cross and follow after Me is not worthy of Me. He who finds his life will lose it, and he who loses his life for My sake will find it.*
> **Matt 10:34-39 NKJV**

This might be some justification for living in a monastic community, however, I believe the true meaning behind this verse lays in the hidden path of detachment.

One can be geographically removed from your loved ones, friends, and all your possessions, but your heart and mind can be filled with them, every hour of every day.

John poses this question in his work, you might renounce all, but are you in exile, are you an alien in this world?

The real question we ask ourselves as we pursue a lifestyle of detachment, will be about our attachment to the world, about our own pleasures and our own preferences. Put another way; "are we predisposed by our pain and pleasure mode of living carnal lives, based on the needs, likes and dislikes of the soul, and body?"

Since we have received a new soul, surely our own ideas of what is acceptable and what is not, should be measured by the divine word of God, and the company of the saints in the church, not our own "taste buds."

Scripture clearly says, "taste and see that the Lord is Good." This process of tasting and seeing then, is a process inspired by the Holy Spirit to re-organize and re-calibrate our sense of pleasure, and our sense of perception.

THE PRACTICE OF DETACHMENT

A state of being objective or aloof. The practice of detachment aids us to develop the ability to look at a situation or circumstance less subjectively and existentially and more objectively, based on a less personal viewpoint.

This idea had its origin in Eastern religion and thought systems, however, the concept in Christianity is translated from the Eastern Orthodox church, as "watchfulness," Philokalia.

The purpose is to cultivate inner calmness and a relaxed state of suppressing the passion of the soul. In some sense, this is translated from the Greek word "Apatheia," which then moves to the English word "indifference" or a stoic view towards life, a quality displayed by a sage or spiritual master.

All these ideas find some expression in Ignatian spirituality and the ideas of Meister Eckard in Christianity.

Detachment practiced understands that God speaks to us in many ways:

- Metaphors
- Dark sayings
- Serendipities
- Epiphanies
- Theophany

When we look at these different methods of divine interaction with humanity, we understand the way of interaction is based very much on the specific person.

We understand that God speaks to us, based on the way we perceive reality, the way we understand ourselves and our context.

The language of the divine, adapts based on the person being spoken to; we will often notice something, and realize that God is saying something to us because we understand there is a meaning attached to the actions of the persons, and situations.

Detachment then is the place where we become more mature, we do not attach meaning to everything. When we hear or dream about strange things, we do not attach **our** meaning, we allow the situation to speak, we allow the atmosphere to be self-subsistent, and existent, we allow God to speak to us.

One of the many things detachment teaches us is to disengage from the outcome of the event, to focus on the moment, the present, the very existence of this moment. As you read this sentence, you focus on each word, not just thinking about the end of this sentence, and the resolution of ideas, but rather the ability to enjoy something based purely on the mere happening, or happenstance.

Detachment is not having a "don't care" attitude, but rather an all-care attitude, where there are no specifics any longer. This fact of identification, and personification, builds an awareness of our own identity, and links the situation or the idea to ourselves. If we refrain from this behavior, our natural inclination to make something ours, the situation becomes more pliable.

Let us explain this with an example: as you look at your mobile phone, imagine dropping it to the ground! What happened?! You had an emotional response to the phone hitting the floor. The reason you had this response, is that you link the phone to yourself, although this inanimate object has no physical link to your body or your emotions. The idea that it falls, and might get damaged, creates an emotional and physical response in you. You have identified yourself with the mobile phone and made it "my" phone.

The practice of detachment builds an ability to observe our own behavior as if based on a third party, seeing how we react to situations, without judging our actions, without correcting any patterns, it helps us to understand the impact of our actions on others.

This objective view of ourselves changes the very behavior because our inner eye engaging in seeing, builds an alternative narrative, that does not link to our identity, because our behavior is sometimes learned responses, not the real actions of a free person.

Detachment implores us to be completely clear and still, silent, without disruption, like the sea of glass, this means the emotions are under control, the reflection of the soul is correct, and un-interrupted, and hence, you sit on the throne of your life, reigning over your life, without the fear and emotional response.

The art of reflection is the art of angle, it depends on your observation angle, what your resulting observation will be.

If we create a space of true reflection, a place of detachment, where the emotions do not disrupt the patterns of water in the body, and the realms of God. Our ability to "see" and judge correctly is greatly increased by our ability to look at the situation less attached.

When trying to gain an understanding of detachment, we build a place of rest inside our hearts, a true rest that is not linked to action, or in-action, but a place of quiet silence where movement is not needed for meaning, only being.

We must assume that Adam had a sense of detachment, as he spoke the animals into creation with God, he was active in terms of labor, yet in-active in terms of striving and perspiration of sweat. We know the Levitical priesthood could not enter the tabernacle with sweat, they needed to have processes of cleaning, signifying that the labor of man is not needed in the temple of God, only pure existence.

We understand also that work in itself is not evil yet striving to attain something becomes an issue. This complete place of rest, mixed with the sense of detachment from outer circumstances, or the cares of this world, builds within us an ability to observe the Creator at work in creation. His light touch pulsed in and out of materiality, and showing His divine provision, and energetic flow, slowly seeping into creation, mixing with materiality, from the world of emanation, to birth the desires of His divine plan.

The practice of detachment, or watchfulness, would require a keen awareness of the movement of the soul, understanding the inner man, and how the soul responds to different stimulus from the spiritual dimensions.

We already know that the soul is impacted by God, through the work of the Holy Spirit, yet we do not fully understand this supernatural working of divinity, on the human heart.

How is the soul transformed by this gazing into the beauty of God, what is the process of metamorphosis that moves the soul from one state of being, to a completely new place of being?

The soul learns to simply watch, be conscious of change, the mere act of observation solidifies the change, and brings quicker metastasis of the soul to bear.

PRACTICAL EXERCISES

One way to practice this would be sitting in front of a grandfather clock, just watching the minutes on the clock, without telling the time.

The grandfather clock, with its bells and pendulum is sometimes easier because the moment of time is easier to conceptualize when the pendulum is moving in a rhythmical way.

The progression of time, slowly moving from the current moment to the moment in the future, then becomes more apparent, the hard part of the exercise, is not to tell the time, not to measure, but only observe.

When the observer only observes the clock, without the natural inclination to mark the time passed, or the time to come, a practice of objectivity is the result.

Try this at home, write down your thoughts after the exercise. It might help to set an alarm clock in the next room, to force your mind to focus on the practice, and not just wait for the period you have set aside for this exercise to be completed.

Detachment from our unhealthy need for things to belong to us and extend our being outside of ourselves into a state of being where observing and awareness sharpens our senses to explore a deeper relationship with God.

(Ignatian Cross)

EXAMEN

A devotional exercise involving reflection on and moral evaluation of one's thoughts and conduct, typically performed daily. (Oxford)

INFLUENCERS OF EXAMEN

"For it is not knowing much, but realising and relishing things interiorly, that contents and satisfies the soul."

— Ignatius of Loyola

Ignatius Loyola was a Catholic Jesuit Priest born in 1491 in Azpeitia, at the castle of Loyola in today's Gipuzkoa, Basque Country, Spain. The blacksmith's wife adopted Ignatius as his mother died soon after his birth and thus María de Garín became his mother.

He joined the military at the age of 17 and was known as a clavier, brash young man, with an affinity for dressing well, and spending time with too many ladies. Ignatius committed many violent crimes at that time but avoided the law due to his station in life.

In 1509 Ignatius started his military career formally, where he grew as a natural leader with a diplomatic flair. He injured his leg at the Battle of Pamplona in 1521.

During his long recovery period, he was only able to read the scriptures, and other spiritual works, as the hospital was administrated and staffed by the church. While reading the works, De Vita Christi, of Ludolph of Saxony he experienced a conversion. This work would later influence his own writing and his spiritual path.

Ignatius started his path of devotion at the Santa Maria de Montserrat. After a time, he walked down the mountain from the monastery to a town called Manresa where he begged for a few months, volunteered at the local hospital, and spent 7 hours a day practicing meditation and developing his spiritual exercise in the cave close to the town.

During 1524 and 1535 Ignatius studied at various institutions completing his Master of Arts degree in 1535. In 1539 Ignatius founded the Society of Jesus with his 2 friends, Peter Faber, and Francis Xavier. This was officially recognized by the Pope, and Ignatius was installed as the Father General by the Jesuits.

Ignatius dispatched his friends to create educational intuitions across Europe, and by doing this converting the population as missionary educators. Juan de Vega started a Jesuit college in Messina which proved to be a huge success and used this as a prototype elsewhere.

Ignatius died from malaria in July 1556, in Rome, he is currently buried at Church of the Gesù. His work regarding Examen has influenced a whole movement and practice centered around the idea of examen.

EXAMEN

The aim of the Examen practice is to involve God in our busy lives, it is a practice created for busy people, not somebody with lots of time on their hands.

We are told to pray ceaselessly, or never-ending prayer, however, this seems an impossible task, unless you remove yourself from the world, and only pray.

What would happen if there was a way to pray for just a few minutes during your day, finding a sacred space, or a quiet place in your office, where you could be alone, and quietly, silently speak to God, and involve Him in the details of your life.

We know God is always present with us, but what would life feel like if we allowed God to climb into our lives, "boots and all," If His presence would permeate our daily moments, if we could share the taste of a great sandwich with Him, or the smell of great coffee, what would it feel like if God really became our best Friend, nor just the silent onlooker?

This practice answers this call, to help us become friends with God, continuously, as our awareness focuses on making Him part of our lives.

Granted you will not always feel goosebumps, or that holy awe moment, but that is not all that "real" relationship is anyway. Let us ask God to be part of our lives, and then build disciplined ways of creating that space in our real-life diary, on our mobile phones, putting alarm reminders on in lunch times, and really spending time with Him.

If we prioritize the divine in our daily routine, He will prioritize us in the big moments of life, and like David, we will be called, "a Friend of God."

FIDELITY TO EXAMEN

Why do we practice the Examen, or why do we practice any method you might ask, is God not spontaneous, should we not just do things as life flows and moves?

Let us be honest with ourselves, we would never have enough time to spend with God, if we just let our lives lead us by the nose. The very nature of life to create movement of priorities, so in simple terms we become busy with normal life, without noticing the passing of time.

You will often hear people say at the end of the year, "time has flown by, where has the year gone"? This is a simple admission, by the person that they did not measure their time, or their life, they allowed everything around them to dictate their reality and were swept along without coming to a rest and deciding, choosing how to spend their time. Are we not a lot like this ourselves?

Any prayer or devotional practice helps us build routine and discipline into our lives, and the moment we repeat these actions consistently, it creates a certain neural pathway, a system of routine, that helps us build a lifestyle of spiritual growth and reality.

By actively pursuing the Christian spiritual life, we make the spiritual world part of our thinking, and part of our life, and thus we become changed in our nature, and our character.

The awakened believer, walking in daily prayer practice, can anticipate the movement of God in creation, to ride the winds of change, and experience the fulfillment of a relationship with the Creator God, which make miracles happen within the mundane.

As we become more aware of the soft wind of God, blowing the leaves of time and moments in our days, we become people of gratitude, living a life thankful for the relationship we can have with the Holy Spirit in our lives.

Those who do not put aside time, and schedule time with their spiritual life, become dull in their hearts. Over time, they will notice the undisciplined disciple strays often from the path of purity, their lives become a wandering meandering, with little progress.

Why would we consider a life well lived, without the movement of God inside our hours, without the intentional connection with the divine. Our modern society has grown so disconnected due to the demands on our time, we have forgotten the relational nature of humanity.

Any relationship requires time, and activity, clear focused attention, nobody likes to have friends that hardly listen to them and hear their needs. We all want companions with big ears, big hearts, and pure agendas, wanting only our friendship and our love, for the sake of sharing life.

These friendships are hard to find, few people have friends like these, the privilege of knowing somebody like this would change your whole life, and loneliness would be a long-lost memory.

We have a friend like this, the Holy Spirit, waiting, silently listening, for the movement of you, the time you make, and the time you take, to get to know Him.

THE PRACTICE OF EXAMEN

The process of practicing Examen has a few major steps. We will look at each one of these and how they can be explored into a spiritual process. We will move on to understand what the whole looks like after explaining the process.

The aim of the process is to discern with God, where God is active in our life, taking note of His active participation, understanding God has a vested interest in us as His children, living a life that testifies for Him.

The practice of Examen is not really an alone standing contemplative action, but a true lifestyle of consistently longing to see the divine operate in our lives.

All spiritual exercises require discipline, the more we practice, the more we will want to do the exercises, the more we let it slip, the less we will start again, and the more momentum is required to get us practicing again.

As we grow in this practice, we might get bored with it, instead of giving up, and throwing in the towel, just pick another practice, try something different, it might not help with the need to push ourselves to set time apart, but it will inspire us to try other things, until we find something that works for us, in that time and space of our life.

The idea with this practice is to spend 15 minutes twice a day, the suggested time is on lunch time and just before dinner. Part of the Examen, is an examination of the waking hours of our day, so at lunch, considering the hours from last night after dinner to 1pm, and then the second examen is done just before dinner, examining the hours between 1pm and 6pm.

The Examen is structured for busy people, and for us in our busy lives, if twice a day is too much, then only do one session. Try to keep it short and sweet, to make sure the practice becomes part of your life, it will require discipline, however, the aim of the Examen is to draw the presence of Christ into your life.

METHOD

The method of Examen can be divided into the following categories for the purpose of understanding the flow of the process that one needs to go through for Examen to have an impact on one's life.

We look at these categories as points of reflection, almost like rest stops along the path of Examen.

- **Transition**
  Become aware of the presence of God, and His eyes upon you as you begin the practice.

- **Gratitude**
  Take note of the gifts that God's love has given you today and thank God for them.

- **Petition**

    Ask God to give you understanding and strength that will help this examen be fruitful beyond your own ability or capacity.

- **Review**

    Imagine holding God's hand; review the day, look for stirrings and trigger points, even thoughts that God has given you today.

    Also look for trigger points where the enemy tried to trigger emotional reactions, or spiritual stirrings.

    Review your reaction to the divine movement, and the less divine moments: How did I respond to the evil one, both in my choices, and my actions?

- **Forgiveness**

    Ask God for forgiveness, knowing God has respect for you, and heals you from even the wrong choices you made, and removes the burdens from your heart.

- **Renewal**

    Look with God toward tomorrow, plan with God how you are going to live and act, knowing the loving kindness and desire from God to see you succeed.

- **Transition**

    Become aware again of God's presence inside your heart, and being, and in prayer conclude and close the Examen.

Because the time spent doing this is also important, a quick tool for remembering the focus of the practice through the following way:

- Relish   - The good moments, and the gifts of today.
- Request - The Holy Spirit to lead the review of the day.
- Review   - Take time to think of the past few hours.
- Repent   - As God for forgiveness for mistakes and wrong decisions.
- Resolve - Make a commitment to do better tomorrow.

There are some foundational questions of this method that we can ask ourselves as we move from the various points of reflection that can help the process:

- Where have I come from?
- Who am I?
- Where am I going?
- How do I get there?
- What do I really want along the way?

Some tips for your practice:

- Find a small A5 journal, and keep a journal of your Examen, "Spiritual Status Update," keep your entry less than 130 characters.
- Journal suggestions:
    o I am really upset about…
    o I am scared about…
    o Considering…, was it as bad as I expected?
    o I feel upset or hurt about…
- Make sure the practice is a prayer, not just mental effort, by doing the following:
    o Ask God to lead your practice.
    o Talk to God, do not just talk to yourself.
    o Listen for God's voice, look at God's reaction, use your imagination.
- Develop your own start and finish ritual; this creates sacred space in your daily routine and helps to focus the mind from a busy day. Examples:
    o Say the "Our Father" before you start.
    o Light a candle when you start and blow it out when you finish.
    o Ring a prayer bowl, or bell when you start or finish.
- Do not get bogged down in your own sin and shortcomings, if you spend all your time naval gazing, you will not lift your heart and head to the people around you who need your love

and care. God forgives sin, He needs us to forgive ourselves and move on.

An example of a practice can be described as follows:

- **STEP 1** - 2 minutes

    'Be still and know I am God'
    Pray for light so that I see and hear what God wants.

- **STEP 2** - 2 minutes

    Thank God for the gifts received:
    1...
    2...
    3...

- **STEP 3** - 4 minutes

    What spoke to me of God?
    Traces of God's presence?
    Love, kindness, generosity, peace, patience, joy, self-control?
    What lifted my spirits?
    Where did that lead me?

- **STEP 4** - 4 minutes

    Signs of God's absence?
    Apathy, lack of consideration, meanness, agitation, impatience, gloom, self-indulgence?
    What dampened my spirits?
    Where did that lead me?

- **STEP 5** - 3 minutes

    Sorrow and renewal.
    Tomorrow ... pitfalls to avoid?
    Forewarned is forearmed!

(Huguenot Cross)

"GLOSSOLALIA" & "XENOLALIA"

CHAPTER 11

Speaking in tongues, also known as glossolalia, is a practice in which people utter words or speech-like sounds, often thought by believers to be languages unknown to the speaker. (wiki)

Xenolalia is the phenomenon in which a person can speak or write in a language they could not have acquired by natural means. (wiki)

INFLUENCERS OF GLOSSOLALIA & XENOLALIA

And when the day of Pentecost was fully come, they were all with one accord in one place. And suddenly there came a sound from heaven as of a rushing mighty wind, and it filled all the house where they were sitting. And there appeared unto them cloven tongues like as of fire, and it sat upon each of them. And they were all filled with the Holy Ghost, and began to speak with other tongues, as the Spirit gave them utterance.

Acts 2:1-4 KJV

How amazing would it have been to witness this first outpouring of the Holy Spirit and the speaking of tongues, for this practice of building up your spirit was given directly by the Holy Spirit and thus the Holy Spirit can be viewed as the first "influencer" of this practice.

Naturally, the disciples present were the executors of the practice and we honour them for spending that time in the upper room, seeking God after Jesus ascended to heaven.

One of my favorite Saints, Hildegard of Bingen is a good example of xenolalia. She had the gift of visions and prophecy and is reported that she was able to speak and write in Latin without having learned the language. She lived in the 12th century in Germany.

Edward Irving was a minister in the Church of Scotland during the 19th century. He is considered as fundamental to the Catholic Apostolic Church foundation. In his writings, he refers to a woman who would "speak at great length, and with superhuman strength, in an unknown tongue, to the great astonishment of all who heard, and to her own great edification and enjoyment in God." Edward further stated that "tongues are a great instrument for personal edification, however mysterious it may seem to us."

The aim of this chapter is not to discuss the theological differences that currently exist in Christianity about this practice, the mere separation of dogmatic and doctrinal separation will not exist in the future as the post-modern belief system removes the need for these crude intellectual separations.

We understand the dogmatic and denomination beliefs in cessation and other theological systems that debate and differ on the application and belief in these gifts. I am not endeavoring to continue this debate here, rather merely to show these existed in the church at large before we started negating these practices to certain denominations or thought systems we prefer.

INTRODUCING GLOSSOLALIA & XENOLALIA

We will be discussing the practice of Glossolalia as a devotional and contemplative practice, enabling the believer to grow spiritually and experience ecstatic states of higher awareness and consciousness.

We know that the belief in Glossolalia, or more commonly known as speaking in tongues, is a commonly held belief in most Charismatic and Pentecostal denominations, attributed to the baptism of the Holy Spirit.

The core verse used is here is *Acts 2:4, "And they were all filled with the Holy Spirit and began to speak in other tongues as the Spirit gave them utterance."*

Before we discuss this practice in modern times, it might be more prudent to also discuss some definitions of the different terms.

The three different Greek words up for discussion in this area is:

- **Akolalia**: a speaker speaks in one language and the hearer hears in his own language (or one he understands)
- **Glossolalia:** a speaker speaks in a language that has no correspondence to a known language
- **Xenolalia:** a speaker speaks in a known (foreign) language unknown to him

Now before we discuss the theological considerations, let us start with some history unknown to most in the church today.

In the 5th Century St Patrick spoke about the Holy Spirit speaking in or praying in a different language unknown to himself.

In the 12th Century St. Hildegard von Bingen as mentioned above spoke and wrote in Latin, some would say this would then represent "Xenolalia." Our third definition represented above in some form. In 1215 in the vita of Hadewijch, she describes the Cistercian and Victorine monasteries developed highly advanced devotional practices and these charismatic gifts included vision, prophecy glossolalia and jubilation.

In 1265 Thomas Aquinas wrote about the gift of speaking in tongues for the purposes of converting others what we would describe as "Akolalia" or the ability to speak to others, as also mentioned in the biblical passage in Acts, Thomas considers this still to be available to those called to this missionary vocation.

THE PURPOSE OF GLOSSOLALIA

Why do we pray in a language we don't understand? It seems as if different languages have brought division into humanity ever since Babel and the separation of the people into different tribes and tongues. To answer this question, we will look at the importance and place that glossolalia has in our faith.

The first thing that happens when the Holy Spirit is poured out on the church, is the ignition of this new language, a spiritual linguistic pattern is birthed into the earth once more.

This divine linguistic didactic removes the faculty of intellectual pride from man, since the mind is unfruitful in this instance, the divine fruit of spiritual ecstasy and union is reconstituted in the human soul.

The receptacle of the human soul is reconfigured to become as Christ has said, "my house shall be a house of prayer for all nations." In essence, the temple of man's body, as the dwelling place of God's worship, this temple is inaugurated with the removal of the self-elevated ego of humanity.

God is thus worshiped "in Spirit and in Truth," for the first time on the Holy mountain of divinely expressed worship, without the sweat of the priest, humanity. The human cognition is removed, and the worship of God, by God interacting with the co-working soul, surrendering the perception of divinity, only to become a vessel of divine worship via the language of the Holy Spirit.

In the Acts account, the people recognize their different languages in the mouths of people who never learned their native tongue. Jews speak every language yet never learn their meaning.

The church becomes a "house of prayer for all nations" divinely orchestrated by the praying of the Holy Spirit inside the temple of humanity, completely surrendering their will and ego to allow God to be God, All in All.

The offensive co-opting of the human intellect, bypassing the cognitive processes and generative ability of man to create meaning, and thus allowing the divine God, to speak once more into creation, not as an outsider, creating, but as a co-creator, inhabiting the body of man, speaking into creation mysteries untold, unseen, and uncompressible to the human mind.

A complete gift of grace and mercy, the language of angels, and the language of man, co-existing in the soul and mouth of man. God "ordaining praise from babes," who have no generative ability to express the mystery of God, a complete ecstasy, enraptured by the beauty of the eternal God.

If man was never meant to communicate using audio, but communicating via light interface, as it is in heaven currently, the reintroduction of this prayer language, is then an initial action to restart the process of helping humanity towards being restored as temples of light emission.

When we pray in tongues, we are essentially reconfiguring our body and our mind, into the mysteries of God. These mysteries cannot be expressed in human language due to the materiality that is trapped in the meaning of all languages.

> *"No eye has seen, no ear has heard, and no mind has imagined what God has prepared for those who love Him."*
>
> **1 Corinthians 2:9 NIV**

We understand that God's limitless ability to create and help humanity to evolve into higher levels of awareness means a new language is needed.

When computers were created, part of the invention process was the development of programming code that could translate the ideas of the programmer into the machine process of executing the programming code.

Essentially a whole new language system needed development, and many programming languages were created, the same applies to the next evolution of man into a space-faring race, once again, new terms, ideas and concepts will need to be communicated.

The process of praying in tongues simulates this process and helps us develop a spiritual understanding in our being, which is later activated when we have the knowledge and understanding.

Some call this "Praying in the Spirit,", however, if this is the case, the Spirit has no time and space linked to it, hence this praying then becomes praying the mysteries of God into existence by uttering spiritual realities, we cannot cognitively grasp yet, but for now God is preparing us.

THE PRACTICE OF GLOSSOLALIA

Before we start this path of discovery on how to attain the gift of Glossolalia, we assume you have a mentor or spiritual director who can already, "speak in tongues." If this is not the case, there are a few options that you can do. Firstly, you can find a Charismatic or Pentecostal type church in your area and ask them to pray for you. You do not need to attend their church or share their belief systems to partake in the gift of the Holy Spirit.

If this option seems too extreme for you to choose, you can take the longer route and ask the Holy Spirit to give you the "gift of tongues" without human intervention, something that is just as possible, and might be more beneficial to your spiritual needs.

To start the practice, sit quietly in a room, and silently start praying in your tongue, you might have done this in the past in different context, but in the contemplative milieu, focus on the Cross or Jesus, or any divine image in your mind.

If the practice of visualization offends you, think on your favorite scripture, or a divine name, as revealed in scripture e.g., YHWH, Elohim, while praying in your tongue.

As you pray, listen to the words coming out of your mouth, the cadence, and intonation, and the different way your body feels while you pray.

Then take some time to pray in the same way, but now change the cadence of the prayer language, try to pray as slowly as possible, slowly intonating and forming the words in your mouth, feel the different ways each word hits your mouth, as you experience the language in your body, because you are understanding what you are praying, the experience and feeling of the language becomes more pronounced.

Now move to a faster pace, pray your tongue as fast as possible, quickly changing the pace, and forming the words as fast as possible, feel the effect in your body, and your atmosphere.

Continue changing the cadence, but also change the intonation of the words, the key in which you speak, or speak louder and softer. You can also sing, chant, or pulse your prayer language. All these techniques of changing speech should make you experience your inner self expanding as you change your way of expressing your prayer language.

It is also possible to have different prayer languages every 10 minutes or so, you should be able to access a different range of sound, almost like you are moving from French to Dutch, or any other 2 languages, the sound should be drastically different.

All these exercises can be done, while the mind is focused on a specific outcome, or direction, one is able to focus on the Cross, however, as the exercise intensifies the ability to think about a specific contemplative object, or divine revealed name becomes harder.

Allow yourself to also experience your breathing, and your whole body, focusing on the feeling of the practice on your body, and how the practice affects your whole being.

If you get bored with praying in your prayer language, you can attempt to write down what you hear yourself pray phonetically, this brings a whole new dimension to your practice, as you now need to distinguish the different sounds you are saying.

Put some worship music on in the background, to help your mind focus on something else, as your prayer language continues.

Prolonged praying this way might help you interpret or understand the scriptures you are contemplating differently, it is sometimes helpful to journal and write your understanding of a verse down, and then pray for some time, while contemplating a verse.

Afterwards, you can write down how you now understand the scripture and how your understanding has changed while in the practice of praying.

Moving around might help you focus on your prayer practice, due to your mind not being involved in the prayer practice, it helps to find other alternative ways to keep the mind focused, some contemplatives walk in patterns of 8 or eternity, allegorically joining the Abrahamic sacrifice, and metaphorically reenacting the encounter mentioned in Genesis.

Others choose some divine patterns or geometric symbolism, to help the mind contemplate the underlying meaning, e.g., the Celtic cross, or the Celtic knot symbolizing the trinity. Praying in your prayer language as you walk the pattern on the floor, using your body and your mind to focus on the hidden meaning behind the actions.

Lastly, it is sometimes helpful to use music in other languages to pray with, the sound of other nations worshiping God, and then praying with this worship, helps you to encounter the God above language and ethnic separation. It also helps to use this technique when praying for other nations, to use their indigenous language, in the context of worship, to encounter the cultural frequency and linguistic patterns.

Language is in its nature an expression of the divine, God created the world by speaking and we were given the same power in our words. Knowing this gives us the choice between life and death as scripture also states. What an incredible responsibility God has given us. How can we then not choose life!

(St James Cross)

BREATHWORK

Breathwork is a modern term for various breathing practices in which the conscious control of breathing is said to influence a person's mental, emotional, or physical state, with a claimed therapeutic effect. (wiki)

INFLUENCERS OF BREATHWORK

"It is not out of place to teach [seekers] to bring their intellect within themselves by means of their breathing". Therefore, it is reasonable to, "recommend them to pay attention to the exhalation and inhalation of their breath, so that while they are watching it, the intellect too, may be held in check. This control of the breathing may, indeed, be regarded as a spontaneous consequence of paying attention to the intellect; for the breath is always quietly inhaled and exhaled at moments of intense concentration, especially in the case of those who practice stillness, both bodily and mentally."

– Saint Gregory Palamas

Although we will not be looking at individual influencers of breathing and Christianity, it is ingrained in the very practice of contemplation that one uses the breath as a means to focus and to remain still.

As illustrated above in the sayings of Saint Gregory Palamas, the very act of breathing brings the mind into a place of engagement that is not unnatural. The mind can easily use breathing as the method of silence as it is one of the natural functions within the body. It also assists in becoming conscious of the working of the body.

BREATHWORK

When a baby is born, we wait anxiously until that first breath is taken and the baby cries. It is the most beautiful sound and celebrated because that breath signifies the life within that baby.

Breathing is our common denominator, we all breathe. We, however, become so busy and unconscious of our own being, that we take breathing for granted. Let us then take a moment before we start; breathe deeply and slowly and remember to exhale deeply. Again. Good work!

This chapter is an introduction to breathing as part of meditation, breathwork, why breath is important, understanding the different types of breathing, and how this affects our consciousness and awareness of the spiritual dimensions.

There are excellent books and resources available for those who want to delve deep into this. We also need to be aware that some breathwork practices are expressly not Christian and should not be practiced by Christian believers.

When starting something new that can influence the body one must make sure to do some research about the medical risks, and how to go about the process. It is always better to practice breath work for the first few times in a group, to familiarize yourself with the different responses of your body, and to help you understand what is normal and what is dangerous.

Most of our breathing is done without even thinking about it. We, as a society, had a rude awakening in 2020 when the COVID-19 pandemic hit the nations and suddenly, our breathing became important again. Thousands of people lost their lives because their oxygen levels dropped dramatically; the whole world stopped because our breathing got interrupted by this awful evil sickness, that will remain part of human history forever.

During this time though, we learned that out breath was important; we became aware and fully awake to our breath with a heightened consciousness. Not only those who contracted the virus, but all of us as we daily wore our masks. Suddenly our breath was in our face!

We, however, cannot just look at this period with disdain, we need to look at the impact that this development has had on us as a people group; we have been allowed to pause, breathe, and remember.

Because we are born with the ability to breathe, we might think of ourselves as experts on the subject. That is not the case, there is breathing that is good for you, some bad and some others that can even promote healing and health. So, we need to discuss breathing to understand the different aspects, then un-learn bad habits of natural breathing and re-learn how to breathe again.

We are not just learning techniques and methods, we are learning how to live, understanding the complex gas balance that exists in our bodies, that enables us to be fruitful and productive members of society with less stress, and more consciousness.

There are 5 major types of breathwork categories:

- Daily Breathwork—fast learning techniques to change your current emotional or body framework (Sleeping and Energy Systems)

- Fix your Breathing Methods—techniques that change your breathing patterns and affect your quality of life (Diaphragm Breathing)

- Peak Performing Breathwork—any speaking or acting techniques, peak performance athletes

- Soul Breathing—Buteyko, Wim Hof Method

- Spiritual Breathing Systems—Rebirthing, Holotropic Breathwork, Transformational Breathing, Biodynamic Breathing, Pranayama Yogic Breathwork

We will discuss some of the methods I believe have more middle of the road systems, and patterns of breathing that could integrate with Christian values.

BREATH IN THE BIBLE

The role of breathing in prayer is almost as important as prayer itself. We know God created Adam, breathed into him, and in so doing created a cycle of breathing that has not stopped since all those millions of years ago.

We see the word breathing mentioned 39 times in the bible, mostly implying somebody is alive, and able to breathe. The Hebrew concept of breathing denotes somebody being alive, they did not share our medical understanding of being "brain dead" as the end of life. To the ancients, breath meant life.

Scriptures that would show this as an example is **Psalm 33:6** *"By the word of the Lord the heavens were made, And by the breath of His mouth all their host."*

What is important to note is the change of breath in meaning from the Old Testament to the New Testament.

The breath God breathed was divine, the very breath of God animated Adam's dead body into life, so since God's breath was shared with Adam, surely our breath has some traces of divine resonance.

Jesus also breathed on His disciples in **John 20:22** – *"And when he had said this, he breathed on them and said to them, 'Receive the Holy Spirit.'"*

The word used here in Greek is "Emfusao," which has provided many biblical scholars with some questions about what Jesus meant when He said, "Receive the Holy Spirit."

This is not the same word used in the Hebrew Roach. We see in **1 Corinthians 15:45**: *"And so it is written, the first man Adam was made a living soul; the last Adam was made a quickening spirit."* KJV

Why did Jesus choose to breathe on them as opposed to spitting at them, or sneezing over them? Jesus chose to breathe, just like God the Father breathed on humanity, to re-animate their hearts, and prepare them for divine encounter.

The contention is that the first breath of God made Adam a living soul. The breath of Jesus after His resurrection was a breath of a man, who overcame death, and was thus breathing immortality and change into their being.

This breath of Jesus reconfigured their beings to understand the scriptures, and made them "quickening spirits," changing the very nature of their being into a higher dimension of creation, not just Adamic, but being "new creations." The breath of Jesus elevated their bodies above the intrinsic nature of Adam.

As we explore breath, and breathing, as we discover that not all breathing is equal, lets learn to breathe with Jesus, let us focus together, and receive the eternal breath of God, in-filling us with the Holy Spirit.

THE VALUE OF BREATHWORK

There is a huge variety of breathwork techniques, and ways to practice breathwork. We will only look at a few major ideas and practices that I have tried and tested myself. Many of the breathwork modalities have some commonalities and ideas, thus, how they are practiced becomes the differentiating factor.

At a baseline, breathwork is amazingly effective at dealing with anxiety, fear, and stress disorders due to the physiological impact of breathwork on the body through increased oxygen to the brain and reducing the fight and flight survival response.

There are various discussions on hyperventilation, "over-breathing" and other terms in the breathwork world, but do not get bogged down by terminology and all the terms regarding your physiology, one does not need to be a doctor or medical professional to start breathing, you are doing it as you are reading this sentence.

A basic understanding of your body, and how your body responds helps you to deal with some of the changes in your blood, and pulse patterns, however, the barrier to engaging with breathwork should not be your understanding of your body. The aim of breathwork is to help you become aware, and intentional about your breathing, this will then affect your sleeping patterns, and your quality of life.

Apart from the physiological effects, like reducing stress, we are spending more time in silence and meditation, and that deals with the unconscious, and subconscious parts of the mind. Many of the techniques being developed deal with this secondary issue, and how to process the emotional trauma underlying modern humanity.

Breathwork has no direct theological starting point, breathing is a natural process, and your breathing signature is learned at an early age. How we approach breathing is based on our own culture, background, and theological ideas, we come to breath with hands filled with ideas, these ideas affect the breathwork, not the other way around.

Breathwork also has a spiritual implication, as we learn to focus on how we breathe, this focus results in spiritual growth and change. Some practitioners in breathwork believe in using the practice to discover their past lives, and other ideas around reincarnation, I do not share these ideas, and I believe one should be careful to describe memories hidden in the DNA, as past life regression. The process of silence and solitude makes us susceptible to spiritual experiences, however these experiences I would caution needs to be processed with some spiritual direction and guidance.

We can easily become enamored by our own spiritual and psychological metaphors and start charting a path of vain imagination and imaginal journey's, this path can only be traversed with spiritual direction and oversight to allow for a more long-term journey of self-discovery and spiritual growth.

The path within always leads to self-discovery, which then develops into a discovery of the kingdom of God.

BREATHWORK TECHNIQUES

We will be discussing a few breathwork techniques and give pointers on how to get started, however, please feel free to research some of these techniques in more depth or attend an online workshop, a workshop in person, and make sure you do enough medical research before you start.

BASIC COMPONENTS

- Conscious connected breathing: no pauses between the inhale and the exhale.
- Diaphragmatic breathing: active inhale into the belly with relaxed expansion of the chest.
- Relaxed exhale: breathing out is a passive movement (let go).
- Breathing channel: breathe in and out through the same channel.
- **Box Breathing**
    - o   Start at the bottom right of the square
    - o   Breathe in for four counts as you trace the first side of the square
    - o   Hold your breath for four counts as you trace the second side of the square
    - o   Breathe out for four counts as you trace the third side of the square
    - o   Hold your breath for four counts as you trace the final side of the square
    - o   You just completed one deep breath
    - o   Repeat

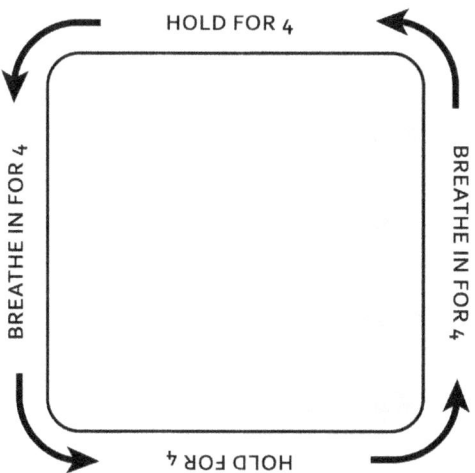

- **Triangular Breathing**
    o   Start at the bottom left of the triangle
    o   Breathe in for three counts as you trace the first side of the triangle
    o   Hold your breath for three counts as you trace the second side of the triangle
    o   Breathe out for three counts as you trace the final side of the triangle
    o   You have just completed one deep breath
    o   Repeat

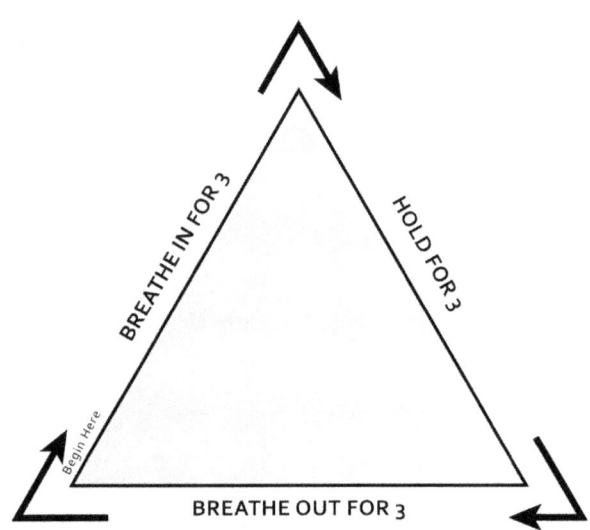

BASIC BREATHWORK EXERCISES

We will now follow a breathwork exercise that calms the mind and helps bring balance and grounding to the body.

Positioning is important as it maximizes the breathing:

- Sit either crossed-legged on the floor or in a chair with your feet flat against the ground.
- Straighten your spine, bring your shoulders back so they are straight, and raise your chest a bit.
- You want your heart in front of your head. Tuck your chin in just enough to flatten the back of your neck.
- Close your eyes.
- Begin by fully inhaling and exhaling, filling your lungs, and allowing your abdomen to fill on the inhale. On the exhale, press your abdominal muscles against your spine to help you fully release the breath.

CONTEMPLATION

Now that you have achieved an optimal position to practice breathwork, let us move into the actual exercises:

Clearing Your Head
Inhale to the count of 4
Exhale to a count of 4
Continue this pattern for 5 to 15 minutes
As you breathe, you may find that you can extend the 4-count to a 5- or 6-count
Do what feels comfortable for you
If you begin to feel winded, just come back to the 4-count box breathing

Inhale for 4

CLEAR THE MIND

Exhale for 4

No More Stress
Inhale to the count of 4
Hold your breath for a count of 4
Exhale to a count of 4
Continue this pattern for 5 to 15 minutes
As you breathe, you may find that you can extend the 4-count to a 5- or 6-count
Do what feels comfortable for you
If you begin to feel winded, just revert to first exercise

Inhale for 4

Hold for 4

RELIEVE STRESS

Hold for 4

Exhale for 4

Deep Chill

Inhale to the count of 4
Hold your breath for a count of 7
Exhale to a count of 8
Continue this pattern for 5 to 10 minutes
Do what feels comfortable for you
If you begin to feel winded,
just revert to first exercise

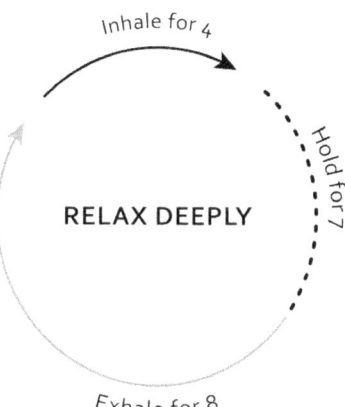

Calm Down

Inhale to the count of 4
Exhale to a count of 6
Continue this pattern for 5 to 10 minutes
Do what feels comfortable for you
If you begin to feel winded, just revert to first exercise

Your breath is amazing, and if you use your breath, as a vehicle for spiritual focus and development, your ability to grow much faster than those around you will be very apparent.

The aim is not competition with somebody next to you, the goal and focus is deeper experience, deeper intimacy and union with the divine, walking into a relationship with God that is real, and helping others around you become closer to Him, as you move in concert with Him, loving and serving humanity around you.

CONTEMPLATION

(Basque Cross)

PSYCHOLOGY & DYING TO SELF

CHAPTER 13

"Very truly I tell you, unless a kernel of wheat falls to the ground and dies, it remains only a single seed. But if it dies, it produces many seeds"
– John 12:24

PSYCHOLOGY

Psychology is the science of mind and behavior. Psychology includes the study of conscious and unconscious phenomena, as well as feeling and thought. (Wiki)

Psychology in the context of meditation must be defined as meditation then influencing the mind and behavior. We can refine the concept even more if we include that we are coming from a Christian perspective in that we are looking to deepen our relationship with God.

How does Christian meditation influence the mind and behavior of the person practicing a contemplative lifestyle? Is there a psychological benefit to these practices and can it be used to influence our mind and behavior in a positive and lasting way as we relate these practices to our relationship with God?

The very reason most people engage with contemplation and meditation is for the benefit of changed behavior and to increase their quality of life. As Christians, we endeavor to use these practices for the very same reasons, although our intent is exclusively focused on our relationship with the divine.

Contemplation and all the practices in this book have a mental impact, when one starts to silence the mind, the underlying unconsciousness and sub-consciousness as well as in some circles the super-consciousness need to be dealt with. As we become still within ourselves, we allow the hidden things in our mind and heart to be revealed. This revealing of the self creates an opportunity to resolve the hurts, fears, unbelief and false sense of self. We become aware of our identity in Christ as we are restored through this process of revealing and healing.

MEDITATION ON DEATH, DYING TO SELF

As Christians we often hear the phrase "dying to self," but we do not really have a grid for the meaning of this phrase because each one of us has a different picture of what dying to self looks like.

The general consensus is a surrendering of your will or denying yourself or then the "self" not being the reason for living anymore. Dying to "self" moves the focus from "self" to the reason God created you.

When we describe "self," are we discussing our ego. This is a focus on identity, and the essence of that identity lies within the reason God created you. We all want to know the "why" of our existence.

> *"For we are God's handiwork, created in Christ Jesus to do good works, which God prepared in advance for us to do."*
> **Eph 2:10, NIV**

> *"For to me to live is Christ, and to die is gain."*
> **Philippians 1:21, KJV**

The surrendering of the will, the understanding of the divine will, our subsequent opposition to the divine will, and the pattern of God to build sonship into the creation of humanity. These ideas are foundational to our ability to "die to self."

Our opposition to God's will is not just the focus of the natural man on sin or evil, but also the carnal man's desire for instant- and self-gratification.

Often our greatest struggle with the divine will is not just a struggle of intention or motivation, but a struggle with timing; God's level of patience with humanity far supersedes our ability to wait, patience in the life of the believer is part of this dying to self.

The dying to self is also the dying to our expectations of God, our ideas of who we should be, expected outcome of success, the ideas about what has meaning, what carries beauty, and our fight with the false self.

Our ideas about everything around us, are shaped by our own preconceptions, misconceptions and pshycological conditioning. When this false self or persona is peeled away, the process feels like dying, because the pain of our identification with this person is complete, we dream the dreams of this "alter ego," we build expectations on life based on the value system derived from the experiences and expectations of the false self.

When we make the conscious decision to surrender our life to God, the process of dying to the self begins as we realize our need for change requires us to re-evaluate who we thought we are.

We become aware of the desire to understand who He made us to be, our destiny, our calling our eternal purpose. Like a light shining before us, pulls us towards this place of longing. Who I am then becomes a very real question and is answered by the immediate reflection of God, like a mirror, showing us, beckoning the greatness in us to spring to life.

During this process we become naked, revealed, and exposed; although only to ourselves in the inner chamber of our time spent with God, but still vulnerable. We need to overcome the fear of being confronted with ourselves and embrace the chance to move from the false self to the true self, whose identity is firmly secured and confirmed by God.

The beauty of becoming who we really are! In this place, the babe born from the womb of eternal creation, before the foundation, echoes with our being, and destroys the edifice we have built.

What is this death then, this death, and resurrection is completed when the resurrected man, is completely devoid of selfish ambition, spiritual tradition, and only holds to one truth, Jesus is Lord, Jesus is King, everything else, matters not. To see Him glorified and elevated in every situation becomes the source of success, the goal of life.

Our human search for significance and legacy often finds their expression in our sense of trying to build generational structures and organizations. We often look to others, who have changed the course of history, and judge their actions based on their history, or what they have created for humanity.

The world is not a better place because you were here, the world is a better place because you allowed yourself to be "hidden in Him," a higher goal than fame or fortune. Some of the most celebrated people in heaven, are not those with the biggest ministries on earth, or the highest achievements on earth, but those who became extravagant in their expression of love.

Why does the women with the bottle of perfume gain such honor in heaven? Is this simply because she anointed the son of God, at the right time and place, or because she spent the most money on God?

Her sole claim to fame is emptiness, her only completed work in life, she became completely empty for Jesus.

Financially she became the poorest person in the room, her life savings generously poured out, every earthly possession in that instant only a fragrance before the Son of Man. Yet her treasure is this: "I loved Him." Her "dying to self" became an eternal living memorial before the God of Creation.

The "anointed one" became the smelly one, the fragranced Son of God, prepared to meet His final hour. She acted with extravagance, instead of fighting about who would sit at the right hand of Jesus, like many of the disciples, she became poor, lost everything in a moment because she found in Him, everything she was ever looking for, the whole goal of her life, was found in that single moment.

The death to self gave life more meaning, the complete surrender, the extravagant dying, led Jesus to lend her His name.

DYING TO SELF – THE PHYCOLOGICAL QUESTION

They triumphed over him by the blood of the Lamb and by the word of their testimony; they did not love their lives so much as to shrink from death.

Rev 12:11 NIV

We know this verse in Revelation so well, but it seems that we have stood still at the first portion of the scripture and not read the second half of this instruction on how to overcome. Yes, by the blood of the Lamb and our testimonies, BUT also by dying to self the laying down of our own lives.

The natural process of centering prayer leads to the contemplation of self, and understanding who you are in this moment, the process of contemplation, is inevitably a process of self-discovery.

Once our minds are focused on the active process of contemplation, the mind is silenced, thoughts are brought to stillness, and without the constant racing of thoughts, the activity of positive and negative thinking comes slowly and deliberately to a complete stop.

This process then becomes the dying of self; by evaluating the nakedness of your soul, reviewing all the masks and personas created over time and awareness of the self.

You become still enough to choose to let go of these additions to your soul that are not benefitting you, the world, and people around you and the plans God has in store for you.

You are allowed to mourn. Mourning brings healing when you allow the tears to reflect the inner struggle of letting go. To mourn somebody you developed, somebody you became, either due to nature, or nurture, the true self, the person you are without preconceived ideas, and moments of false judgements comes to the foreground of your thoughts.

In this moment of unveiling, the moment of realization, the process of acceptance can start, learning to love the "you," without trying to perform according to the expectations of others.

The process of discovery starts here as we allow God, the Holy Spirit, to slowly lead us towards the person He desires us to be, the person Abba Father created, the real, true version of who we are.

Jesus is not intimidated by our humanity, or our lack of perfection, however, the longer we cling to the false persona, the longer this process will take, and the longer our true-life purpose cannot be established on the earth.

The process of contemplation is thus a cardinal point in the growth of the believer, mostly ignored or forgotten by institutional Christianity, robbing us unconsciously of the very tools we need to become the true image and likeness of Jesus.

It is hard to die to your own desires, or own ideas and dreams, if you do not even know who you are, and what you want from life. Through contemplation, you start to create a new narrative to your story, your God-story.

(Coptic Cross)

PHILOSOPHY OF CONTEMPLATION

*"For as he thinks in his heart, so is he. "Eat and drink!"
he says to you, but his heart is not with you."*
– Prov 23:7 NKJV

PHILOSOPHY

Philosophy is the study of general and fundamental questions, such as those about reason, existence, knowledge, values, mind, and language. (Wiki)

Philosophy has been an integral part of humanity for as long as humanity has been able to ask the question WHY. Many influencers have tried to capture the essence of philosophy and our understanding of the field grows every day.

Bringing contemplation into the sphere of philosophy we look at Plato. He thought that through contemplation the soul may ascend to knowledge of the divine. Another philosopher, Plotinus, believed that the highest form of contemplation was to experience the vision of God.

When we approach the philosophy of contemplation there are 4 major areas of discussion:

- The existence of God & and our relationship with divinity
- Epistemology (how do we know what we know)
- The human being (mechanics of being)
- Contemplation as a philosophical practice and endeavor

Let us review epistemology within the philosophy of contemplation as we endeavor to explain and understand the questions that comes from this idea.

EPISTEMOLOGY

Epistemology is the area of philosophy concerned with knowledge. Epistemologists study the nature, origin, and scope of knowledge. The question within epistemology is how do we know what we know?

We look at epistemology in the light of a contemplative lifestyle because within contemplation itself lies a paradoxical point where the knowledge of "knowing" something and "feeling" or "experiencing" something is present when introspection of the soul takes place.

In Epistemology, we almost become the four-year-old that keeps on asking "WHY," until we are exhausted to just think about another answer. This exhaustion will open your heart to the possibility of answers that your perceived ideas would have rejected.

So, let us look at the quest for "WHY"!

CAPPADOCIAN FATHERS

The Cappadocian Fathers were in many aspects the first to develop the Christian Theology mainly to give the intellectual tools and ability to Christians to hold their own in conversations with intellectuals. Their contribution was a knowledge-base that other Christians could use to defend their viewpoints and beliefs.

The collective group known as the Cappadocian Fathers, primarily due to the region being Cappadocia, in modern-day Turkey, where they all come from, and lived, refers to three men.

The three men are:

- Basil the Great (330 – 379)
- Gregory of Nyssa (335 – 395)
- Gregory of Nazianzus (329 – 389)

Let us start with Gregory of Nyssa, and his Epistemology, "theory of knowing," we understand that when discussing the philosophical concepts of contemplation, we need to deal with the question of knowing. How do we know anything? Is what we believe true, and how do we judge what we know to be true?

Gregory's theory of knowing focuses on the life of Moses, and his experiences with God. Gregory looks at the life of Moses, as three distinct theophanies, where he experiences the divine.

The first experience is the "burning bush" moment, where Moses is illuminated to the knowledge of God, and his own purpose in life. He also argues the bible needs to be seen and interpreted as allegory, the only way then is to find God in the metaphor and not the crude literal scriptures, with apparent meaning attached.

The second theophany in the life of Moses, is the "Mount Sinai experience," where darkness is the access point to God, no longer is light an expression of divinity. In this experience, Moses learns that God is ultimately incomprehensible, and our surface-level experience of God, is just an introduction to learn what we try to avoid, our humanity is in essence not able to understand or comprehend the vastness of God.

Man's knowledge of God is now mediated by "spiritual senses," and in some way, God exposes Himself to us, and helps us to understand and know Him as God, our human ability to comprehend spiritual matters seems useless.

> *But the natural man does not receive the things of the Spirit of God, for they are foolishness to him; nor can he know them, because they are spiritually discerned.*
>
> **1 Cor 2:14 NKJV**

The third theophany in the life of Moses is the "Cleft in the Rock" moment, where Moses has a vision of God's glory. The progress of Moses now becomes complete; he is only able to see the "back" of God, as God shelters him from Himself, thus Moses learns the very mystery of God, the complete unknowing knowing of God, the process of understanding is never possible when man tries to understand God, the process is an infinite journey beyond life, and death.

Basil the Great uses the term "physikê theôria" (natural contemplation), where nature and beauty in the material realm are seen as the point of interface between man and God. In essence, man uses creation like a ladder ascending to God. The awe and wonder of creation, according to Basil helps us discover the beauty of the divine and walk with God.

Nature then needs to be contemplated with a mind free from the passions of life. Basil discusses in his writings the purification of the mind, if this process is not undertaken, man's quests to see beyond the natural sensing faculties are merely flights of fancy.

It is clear in Basil's writings the grace of God is required to be free from the "passions" and enter the world of the divine, where contemplation can be attempted without distraction or superstition.

Basil focuses on the mystery of the incarnation of Christ, and by implication God, into human form, this glorification of man, then enables the human being governed by God to access the beauty of God and contemplate His Divine nature.

The end of Basil's thought and life, concluded in Basilian Monasticism, which developed into communities throughout the world, practicing his method of contemplation.

Gregory of Nazianzus is the last of the Cappadocian church fathers that we look at. His focus is on purification and a word used about 374 times in his writings "catharsis," clearly an important concept in his thought.

Gregory believes that the contemplation on God, and with God, leads to transformation, the very nature of this encounter with God, shocks the believer into a changed person. His teaching focuses on the nature of God, as the source of all goodness, and that once the all-encompassing contemplation on the goodness of God is embarked upon, the journey of life becomes clear, God is the source, and everything else becomes trivial in this divine reality.

The splendor of God, the sheer shocking beauty of God, and the only emanation of beauty in creation, then aligns the passions of the person, and brings man into true alignment with God.

Gregory calls humanity into union with God, and then explains in his other teachings, the pursuit of God, the human heart. Bringing into balance the hide-and-seek relationship God has with us, and clearly demonstrating God is in pursuit of humanity, and the salvation of the human soul.

THE ACT OF "UNKNOWING" OR "UN-LEARNING"

The epistemology and the discussion on mystery; how do we know what we know, and how to observe this in spiritual reality is the "unknowing.".

In essence, the question Pontius Pilate asked Jesus "Quis Est Veritas?", refers to "what is truth." This question remains one of the hardest to answer, especially when faced with the mystery of God, as a way of knowing.

What happens when we do not know, when darkness is the only way forward, and the only way to really understand, yet understanding is not present. The way of mystery, what does this mean, when the mind of man has been darkened, and their understanding is then null and void.

We know, mere observation is not comprehension, having observed a scientific experiment being done in the laboratory does not mean one comprehends the advanced chemical knowledge required to re-create the complex experiment again.

The "ray of darkness" sounds like an oxymoron, however, uncreated light has been just that, it does not exist in the created universe. God is light, but His divine light, is not the same light we observe with our natural eyes, the light of God is more complex, more diverse than any existing materiality we now know. Because light is used to observe, which in turn, then creates the sense of knowing.

What would happen if the light were not observed, and the mystery remains what is in essence, a complete mystery, how then can we comprehend. If God understands something, considering that God knows everything, then the light excluding from His divinity, is constantly exploding, creating, and building an atmosphere of observation.

Like an observatory, looking at the stars, plotting their course, the divine gaze of God, does not just look upon the earth, but looks upon all things, and understands, knows, and comprehends all things, always. In some sense this light of God is ubiquitous.

The sound of God, consistently vibrates in creation, holding everything together, this sound of God in one part, holds creation. The light of God, being un-created, and unlimited, then holds the same function elsewhere.

Uncreated space and time, the place where God exists outside creation, outside everything we know, is then framed by God alone. The very frame of God frames the realms and dimensions God exists in, because anything else does not exist, nor has it ever existed.

This is not the eternal or infinite realm, as some would suggest, as both these realms exists in creation, hence the tree of life, the tree in the garden existed as a tree of life, which meant eternal immortality was possible in Eden.

What was not in the garden, was God, God interrupted the pattern of the garden and "dwelt" with Adam. He manifested Himself momentarily in the space He created for Himself and Adam to co-exist in the same place.

INTUITIVE KNOWING

Intuitive knowing becomes the path of knowledge to the believer, although our theories of knowing is all based on our sensory perception, or our cognitive abilities. All religions or belief systems, at some point, demand a "leap of faith," for some belief systems this leap might feel like a giant jump, and for others a more leisurely hop from one space to another.

The fact is, God is not perceived by the instruments of human intellect or understanding. We can grasp the concept of God via our intellectual reasoning, just like nature points to God, so does clear reasoning.

To have a relationship with the divine, like John of the Cross wrote, and so many others, a "dark night of the soul" follows, where all preceptive capabilities cease to access the divine. The intuitive knowing becomes the only sense of God's presence, the instinctive sense that God is never absent, in every situation; Jesus is still "Emmanuel" — God with us.

In this complete darkness of intellect, understanding or sensory input, God feels like He has completely removed Himself from our reality. The agnostic reality enters, God might exist, but if He does, He cannot be reached by man. To cross this bridge, the believer needs to embrace the darkness, and groping through the darkness, allows this knowing to enter the self.

God exist beyond all our own ideas, or humanity, and thus, the spiritual path begins to ascend, and our contemplative path winds deeper into the mountains of spiritual understanding and exploration.

Inside of us starts to flower the divine unknowing, yet surpassing reality, and we come to know God, not as we are, but as God truly exists.

A God made not in our image, giving us pain and pleasure, based on our needs, our humanity, but a God that exists beyond us, that has a relationship with us, and loves us as only God can love the created being He designed to be created before time and space began.

This is the journey of the mystic, the journey you are invited to join, a path that will cost you everything, and then help you to realize you did not really pay anything at all.

All becomes worthless when we gaze into the divine Face of God, and realize all was lost before Him, all is found in Him.

(Constantine Cross)

RECOMMENDED READING PER CHAPTER

Chapter 1 – Contemplative Prayer
- Gregory the Great
- Saint Ignatius Brianchaninov
- Ignatius Loyola
- Henri de Tourville

Chapter 2 – Quietism
- Miguel de Molinos
- George Fox
- Madame Guyon

Chapter 3 – Hesychasm
- St. John Climacus
- St. Nicephorus the monk
- Gregory Papamus
- Elder Joseph the Hesychast
- Nikitas Stithatos

Chapter 4 – Centering Prayer
- Thomas Keating
- Thomas Merton
- William Meninger
- M. Basil Pennington

Chapter 5 – Lecto Divina
- Pope Guigo I
- Richard Baxter

Chapter 6 – Visio Divina
- John of Damascus

Chapter 7 – Silence & Solitude
- Evagrius Ponticus
- Saint Issac of Syria

- Antony the Great
- Gregory of Sinai
- Isaiah the Solitary

Chapter 8 – Mindfulness
- Theophan the Recluse
- John Main

Chapter 9 – Detachment
- John Climacus
- Jacob Boehme
- Meister Eckhart

Chapter 10 – Examen
- Ignatius of Loyola

Chapter 11 – Glossolalia
- Edward Irving
- Beguines
- Hildegard of Bingen

Chapter 12 – Breathwork
- Saint Dionysius the Areopagite
- Nikitas Stithatos
- Saint Symeon the new Theologian
- Seraphim of Sarov

Chapter 13 – Psychology & Dying to Self
- Theologia Germanica
- Hugo and Richard of St Victor
- Thomas Traherne
- Clement of Alexandria
- Cloud of Unknowing, An Anonymous Christian Mystic
- Pseudo-Dionysius

Chapter 14 – Philosophy of Contemplation
- Gerhard Tersteegen
- Evelyn Underhill

BIBLIOGRAPHY

1) Christian Mindfulness | Peter Tyler | SCM Press 2018|
   ISBN # 978-0-334-05671-3
2) Kenosis in Theosis | Sigurd Lefsrud |Pickwick Publications 2020
   ISBN # 978-1-5326-9370-0
3) Finding Grace at the Center | M Basil Pennington by Skylight Paths Publishing 2007
   ISBN # 978-1-893361-69-0
4) The Path of Centring prayer| David Frenette by Sounds true 2012
   ISBN # 978-1-62203-866-4
5) Practical Mysticism | Evelyn Underhill
6) Word into Silence | John Main by Darton Longman & Todd 1980
   ISBN # 978 1 85311 754 1
7) Thoughts on Solitude |Thomas Merton | Farrar, Straus, and Giroux 1956 |
   ISBN # 9781429944076
8) World without End |Thomas Keating | Bloomsbury 2017
   ISBN # 9781472942487
9) Just This | Richard Rohr by SPCK 2018
   ISBN # 978–0–281–07991–9
10) The Celtic way of prayer | Ester de Waal by Canterbury Press 1996
    ISBN # 978 1-84825-051-2
11) Mindfulness and Christian spirituality | Tim Stead by SPCK 2016
    ISBN # 978–0–281–07486–0
12) In the Stillness Dancing | Neil MaKenty by Torchflame boos 2017
    ISBN # 978-1-61153-204-3
13) Jesus the teacher within | Lawrence Freeman by Canterbury press 2000
    ISBN # 978 1-84825-037-6
14) Meditation for Christians | Bradley Dean Stephan by Smashwords 2001
    ISBN # 0-9706517-0-8
15) Mertons Palace of Nowhere | James Finley by Ave Maria Press 1978
    ISBN # 13 978-0-87793-041-9
16) One Breath at a Time | J Dana Trent by Upper Room books 2018

ISBN # 978-0-8358-1855-1
17) Love is stronger than death | Cynthia Bourgeault by Monkfish publishing 1999
ISBN # 9781939681362
18) The way of the heart | Henry Nouwen by HarperOne Publishing 2016
ISBN # 978–0–06–066330–8
19) Mindful silence | Phileena Heuertz IVP books 2018
20) The Examen prayer | Timothy M Gallagher by Crossroad publishing 2006
ISBN # 978–0–8245–2367–1
21) Apatheia in the Christian Tradition | Joseph H Nguyen | Cascade books 2018
ISBN # 978-1-5326-4516-7
22) Gregory of Nazianzus | Brain Matz | Baker Academic 2016
ISBN # 978-1-4934-0572-5
23) A companion to Mysticism and Devotion in Northern Germany | Elizabeth Anderson by Brill Publishing 2014 | ISBN # 978-90-04-25793-1
24) Breathing from the Heart | Aguirre, Ana María by Montsecortazar Literary agency
ISBN # 978-987-86-4988-7
25) Lectio Divina | Enzo Bianchi | SPCK Publishing 2015 |
ISBN#978-0-281-07334-4
26) Transformed by God's Word | Stephen J Binz |Ave Maria Press 2016|
ISBN#978-1-59471-651-5
27) Opening to God | David G Benner | InterVarsity Press 2010|
ISBN#978-0-8308-6799-8
28) Lectio Divina| Duncan Robertson
29) Lectio Divina the sacred art | Christine Valters Painter | Skylightpaths publishing 2011 | ISBN# 978-1-59473-300-0
30) Breathing as Spiritual Practice | Will Johnson| InnerTraditions Publishing 2019
ISBN# 978-1-62055-687-0
31) When the soul listens | Jan Johnson| NavPress 2017|
ISBN#978-1-61346-686-1
32) Contemplative Prayer a new framework | David Foster | Bloomsbury 2015
ISBN#978-1-4081-8712-8
33) Mindful Silence The heart of Christian contemplation| Phileena Heuertz | IVP Books
34) Armchair Mystic | Mark E Thibodeaux S.J. | Franciscan Media 2019
ISBN# 978-1-63253-288-6

35) Centering prayer and the healing of the unconscious | Merchadh O Madagain
    Lantern Books 2007 | ISBN # 978-1-59056-107-2
36) Exhale | Richie Bostock| Penguin Random house 2020|
    ISBN#978-0-241-4044-3
37) A Practical guide to Breathwork | Jesse Coomer | Midwestern Method
    ISBN# 978-0-578-75801-5
38) Breathe | Mary Birch | Piatkus 2019| ISBN# 978-0-349-42190-2
39) Befriending Silence | Carl McColman | Ave Maria Press 2016
    ISBN # 978-1-59471-615-7
40) The Jesus Prayer | John Michael Talbot| IVP Books 2013
    ISBN#978-0-8308-35775
41) Mysteries of the Jesus Prayer| Norris Chumley| Harper Collins 2011
    ISBN# 978-0-187417-8
42) The Monastery of the heart | Joan Chittister | SPCK publishing 2011 |
    ISBN# 978-0-281-06619-3
43) The Spiritual Guide | Michael Molinos | Seedsowers |
    ISBN# 0-940232-08-1
44) Reimagining the Ignatian Examen | Loyola Press 2015| Mark E Thibodeaux
    ISBN # 978-0-8294-42441
45) The Elder Joseph the Hesychast | Elder Joseph of Vatopaidi |
    ISBN# 978-618-5314-23-1
46) One Breath at a Time | J Dana Trent | Upper Room books 2018
    ISBN# 978-0-8358-1855-1
47) Obedience is life : Elder of Epharaim of Katounakia | Elder Joseph of Vatopaidi |
    ISBN# 978-618-5314-26-2
48) The Edge of Glory | David Adam | Triangle publishing 1985 |
    ISBN # 0-281-04197-0
49) Byzantine Christianity | Averil Cameron | SPCK 2017 |
    ISBN # 978–0–281–07613–0
50) The Golden Cord | Adonijah O Ogbonnaya PHD | Seraph Creative
    ISBN# 978-0-9946974-4-8

ABOUT THE AUTHOR

Kevin Hall is a husband, father, futurist, businessman and pastor. He loves the local church and to see God move in the nations, he is passionate about Africa, and enjoys special moments with his family in South Africa.

Kevin ministers to people searching for the truth of the Gospel, bringing the focus back to the foundations of the Gospel of Jesus Christ.

Kevin founded various ministries during the past few years and successfully handed those ministries over to continue the work that they had started. Kevin currently pastors One House, a virtual church community. He is also the CEO of Savantage, an international events and consulting company.

Kevin's heart is to bring people into the fullness of what Father has intended them to be, moving beyond identity to discovering their divine destiny. Bringing people into the understanding that a personal vibrant interactive relationship with Jesus is possible.

OTHER BOOKS BY THIS AUTHOR

MYSTIC MOTHERS

Have you always wanted to know about the Mystic Mothers who shaped the way we do church and the weird and wonderful things they said and did? Then this delightful edition of an introduction to the Mystic Mothers of the monastic era is the book for you.

You are invited to explore some of the great female Saints like Theresa of Avila, Madam Guyon, Bridget of Ireland and many more in this easy-to-read book with some surprises along the way.

Mystic Mothers include:

- Short background on the Saint
- Extracts from their most popular works
- Personal experiences
- Question for self-study
- Places to make notes

Mystic Mothers takes you on a journey of discovery and transformation about your understanding of the female Saints, their lives, struggles and most of all their love for God. May you be blessed by their lives and find your own experiences along the way.

OTHER BOOKS BY THIS AUTHOR

MYSTIC FATHERS

Amongst all the brilliant, revolutionary, and famous Mystic Fathers of the church through the ages, who would you choose to shape and influence your understanding of spiritual truths?

This thought-provoking edition of an introduction to the Mystic Fathers of the monastic era is the perfect ensemble of well-known and not so well-known pioneers of our faith.

Reading this book introduces you to men like Francis of Assisi, John of the Cross, Benedict of Nursia and many more that invites you to open your heart to them once more.

Mystic Fathers includes:

- Short background on the Saint
- Extracts from their most popular works
- Personal experiences
- Question for self-study
- Places to make notes

Men of God who endured persecution, ridicule, poverty and many more hardships for the sake of the Gospel; for their love of God and their compassion towards people are found within the pages of Mystic Fathers and challenges us to reach deeper into ourselves to meet God anew.

May you be blessed by their lives and find your own experiences along the way.

Contact the Author - Kevin Hall

http://onehouse.co.za

http://savantage.co.za

Seraph Creative is a collective of artists, writers, theologians & illustrators who desire to see the body of Christ grow into full maturity, walking in their inheritance as Sons of God on the Earth.

Sign up to our newsletter to know about future exciting releases.

Visit our website:

www.seraphcreative.org

www.ingramcontent.com/pod-product-compliance
Lightning Source LLC
Chambersburg PA
CBHW071626080526
44588CB00010B/1291